AMERICAN CRIME STORIES

Criminals in the United States of America are much the same as criminals in any other place. They lie, cheat, steal, carry guns, break into houses – and murder people. Sometimes they get caught, sometimes they don't. And some of them have bad dreams for the rest of their lives.

These seven stories by well-known American writers show us the many faces of crime. There are murders of passion, and of revenge; murders that look like suicides or accidents. There is robbery and mugging, fear and hate, love and laziness. There are the innocent and the guilty – but which are which? And there are the detectives: the amateur Louise, who won't accept that her cousin's death was suicide, and who goes looking for a lipstick; and the coolly professional private eye, who knows whose hand is behind the machine guns and hand grenades on a stormy night in Couffignal.

We begin with *Death Wish*, with a man leaning over the Morrissey Bridge late at night – a man with dark thoughts of suicide in his mind . . .

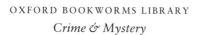

OXFORD BOOKWORMS LIBRARY
Crime & Mystery

American Crime Stories

Stage 6 (2500 headwords)

Series Editor: Jennifer Bassett
Founder Editor: Tricia Hedge
Activities Editors: Jennifer Bassett and Christine Lindop

RETOLD BY JOHN ESCOTT

American Crime Stories

OXFORD UNIVERSITY PRESS

OXFORD

UNIVERSITY PRESS

Great Clarendon Street, Oxford OX2 6DP

Oxford University Press is a department of the University of Oxford.
It furthers the University's objective of excellence in research, scholarship,
and education by publishing worldwide in

Oxford New York

Auckland Cape Town Dar es Salaam Hong Kong Karachi
Kuala Lumpur Madrid Melbourne Mexico City Nairobi
New Delhi Shanghai Taipei Toronto

With offices in

Argentina Austria Brazil Chile Czech Republic France Greece
Guatemala Hungary Italy Japan Poland Portugal Singapore
South Korea Switzerland Thailand Turkey Ukraine Vietnam

OXFORD and OXFORD ENGLISH are registered trade marks of
Oxford University Press in the UK and in certain other countries

ISBN 978 0 19 479253 0

A complete recording of this Bookworms edition of
American Crime Stories is available on audio CD ISBN 978 0 19 479243 1

Printed in China

Illustrated by: Guillaume Decaux/Agent 002 Paris

Word count (main text): 26,500 words

For more information on the Oxford Bookworms Library,
visit www.oup.com/elt/gradedreaders

CONTENTS

ACKNOWLEDGEMENTS

The publishers are grateful to the following for their kind
permission to adapt copyright material:

Knox Burger Associates Ltd for *Death Wish*, copyright ©
Lawrence Block 1967, 1993;

Curtis Brown Ltd for *Death on Christmas Eve* by Stanley Ellin;

The Robert Lantz-Joy Harris Literary Agency Inc for *The
Gutting of Couffignal*, copyright © The Estate of Dashiel
Hammett;

Tanja Howarth Literary Agency for *The Heroine* by Patricia
Highsmith;

The David Grossman Literary Agency for *Ride the Lightning* by
John Lutz, first published in *Alfred Hitchcock's Mystery
Magazine*, copyright © 1984 by Davis Publications Inc;

Meredith Bernstein Literary Agency Inc for *Lazy Susan* by Nancy
Pickard;

Uli Rushby-Smith & Shirley Stewart for *The Lipstick* by Mary
Roberts Rinehart.

The publishers have been unable to trace all the copyright holders
for *The Lipstick* by Mary Roberts Rinehart, but if contacted, will
be pleased to rectify any errors or omissions at the earliest
opportunity.

Death Wish
LAWRENCE BLOCK

The cop saw the car stop on the bridge but didn't think too much about it. People often stopped their cars on the bridge late at night, when there was not much traffic. The bridge was over the deep river that cut the city neatly in two, and the center of the bridge provided the best view of the city.

Suicides liked the bridge, too. The cop didn't think of that until he saw the man get out of the car, walk slowly along the footpath at the edge, and put a hand on the rail. There was something about that lonely figure, something about the grayness of the night, the fog coming off the river. The cop looked at him and swore, and wondered if he could get to him in time.

He didn't want to shout or blow his whistle because he knew what shock or surprise could do to a probable suicide. Then the man lit a cigarette, and the cop knew he had time. They always smoked all of that last cigarette before they went over the edge.

When the cop was within ten yards of him, the man turned, gave a slight jump, then nodded as if accepting that the moment had passed. He appeared to be in his middle thirties, tall with a long narrow face and thick black eyebrows.

'Looking at the city?' said the cop. 'I saw you here, and thought I'd come and have a talk with you. It can get lonely at this hour of the night.' He patted his pockets, pretending to look for his cigarettes and not finding them. 'Got a spare cigarette on you?' he asked.

The man gave him a cigarette and lit it for him. The cop thanked the man and looked out at the city.

'Looks pretty from here,' he said. 'Makes a man feel at peace with himself.'

'It hasn't had that effect on me,' the man said. 'I was just thinking about the ways a man could find peace for himself.'

'Things usually get better sooner or later, even if it takes a little while,' the cop said. 'It's a tough world, but it's the best we've got, and you're not going to find a better one at the bottom of a river.'

The man said nothing for a long time, then he threw his cigarette over the rail and watched it hit the water. He turned to face the cop. 'My name's Edward Wright. I don't think I'd have done it. Not tonight.'

'Something particular bothering you?' said the cop.

'Not . . . anything special.'

'Have you seen a doctor? That can help, you know.'

'So they say.'

'Want to get a cup of coffee?' said the cop.

The man started to say something, then changed his mind. He lit another cigarette and blew out a cloud of smoke. 'I'll be all right now,' he said. 'I'll go home, get some sleep. I haven't been sleeping well since my wife —'

'Oh,' the cop said.

'She died. She was all I had and, well, she died.'

The cop put a hand on his shoulder. 'You'll get over it, Mr Wright. Maybe you think you can't live through it, that nothing will be the same, but—'

'I'd better get home,' the man said. 'I'm sorry to cause trouble. I'll try to relax, I'll be all right.'

The cop watched him drive away and wondered if he should have taken him into the police station. But if you started taking in everyone who thought about suicide, you'd never stop. He went back towards the other side of the bridge. When he reached it, he took out his note-book and wrote down the name, *Edward Wright*. So he would remember what the man meant, he added, *Big Eyebrows, Wife Dead, Thought About Jumping.*

The psychiatrist stroked his pointed beard and looked at the patient.

' . . . no longer worth living,' the man was saying. 'I almost killed myself the night before last. I almost jumped from the Morrissey Bridge.'

'And?'

'A policeman came along. I wouldn't have jumped anyway.'

'Why not?'

'I don't know.'

The endless talk of patient and doctor went on. Sometimes the doctor went through a whole hour without thinking at all, making automatic replies but not really hearing a word that was said to him. *I wonder,* he thought, *whether I do these people any good at all. Perhaps they only want to talk, and need a listener.*

He listened next to a dream. Almost all his patients told him their dreams, which annoyed the psychiatrist, who never remembered having a dream of his own. He listened to this dream, glancing now and then at his watch and wishing the hour would end. The dream, he knew, indicated a decreasing wish to live, a development of the death wish, and a desire for suicide that was prevented only by fear. But for how long?

Another dream. The psychiatrist closed his eyes and stopped listening. Five more minutes, he told himself, and then this fool would leave.

The doctor looked at the man, saw the heavy eyebrows, the expression of guilt and fear. 'I have to have my stomach pumped, Doctor,' the man said. 'Can you do it here or do we have to go to a hospital?'

'What's the matter with you?'

'Pills.'

'Sleeping pills? How many did you take?'

'Twenty,' said the man.

'Ten can kill you,' said the doctor. 'How long ago did you take them?'

'Half an hour. No, maybe twenty minutes.'

'And then you decided not to act like a fool, yes? Twenty minutes. Why wait this long?'

'I tried to make myself sick.'

'Couldn't do it? Well, we'll try the stomach pump,' the doctor said.

It was very unpleasant, but finally the doctor said, 'You'll live.'

'Thank you, Doctor.'

'Don't thank me. I'll have to report this.'

'I wish you wouldn't. I'm . . . I'm under a psychiatrist's care. It was more an accident than anything else, really.'

The doctor raised his eyebrows. 'Twenty pills? You'd better pay me now. I can't risk sending bills to people who may be suicides.'

'This is a fine gun for the price,' the clerk said. 'But for just a few dollars more—'

'No, this will be satisfactory. I'll need a box of bullets.'

The clerk gave him a box. 'Or three boxes for—'

'Just the one.'

The shopkeeper opened a book. 'You'll have to sign there, to keep the law happy.' He checked the signature when the man had finished writing. 'I'm supposed to see something to identify you, Mr Wright. Can I see your driver's license?' He checked the license, compared the signatures, and wrote down the license number.

'Thank you,' said the man.

'Thank *you*, Mr Wright. I think you'll get a lot of use out of that gun.'

'I'm sure I will.'

At nine o'clock that night, Edward Wright heard his back doorbell ring. He walked downstairs, glass in hand, finished his drink and went to the door. He was a tall man with thick black eyebrows. He looked outside, recognized his visitor, and opened the door.

His visitor put a gun in Edward Wright's stomach.

'Mark—'

'Invite me in,' the man said. 'It's cold out here.'

'Mark, I don't—'

'Inside.'

In the living room, Edward Wright stared at the gun and knew that he was going to die.

'You killed her, Ed,' the visitor said. 'She wanted a divorce. You couldn't let her have that, could you? I told her it was

5

dangerous to tell you, that you were nothing but an animal. I told her to run away with me and forget you but she wanted to do the right thing, and you killed her.'

'You're crazy!'

'You made it look like an accident, didn't you? How did you do it? Tell me, or this gun goes off.'

'I hit her.' Wright looked at the gun, then at the man. 'I hit her a few times, then I threw her down the stairs. You can't go to the police with this, you know. They can't prove it and they wouldn't believe it.'

'We won't go to the police,' the man said. 'I didn't go to them at the beginning. They didn't know of a motive for you, did they? I could have told them a motive, but I didn't go, Edward. Sit down at your desk. Take out a piece of paper and a pen. There's a message I want you to write.'

'You can't—'

'Write *I can't go on any longer. This time I won't fail*, and sign your name.' He put the gun against the back of Edward Wright's shaking head.

'You'll hang for it, Mark.'

'Suicide, Edward.'

'No one will believe I was a suicide, note or no note. They won't believe it.'

'Just write the note, Edward. Then I'll give you the gun and leave you to do what you must do.'

'You—'

'Just write the note. I don't want to kill you, Edward. I want you to write the note, and then I'll leave you here.'

Wright did not exactly believe him, but the gun at his head left him little choice. He wrote the note and signed his name.

6

'Just write the note.'

'Turn round, Edward.'

He turned and stared. The man looked very different. He had put on false eyebrows and false hair, and he had done something to his eyes.

'Do you know who I look like now, Edward? I look like *you*.

7

Not exactly like you, of course, but a good imitation of you.'

'You – you've been pretending to be me? But why?'

'You just told me you're not the suicidal type, Edward. But you'd be surprised at your recent behavior. There's a policeman who had to talk you out of jumping off the Morrissey Bridge. There's the psychiatrist who has been seeing you and hearing you talk about suicide. There's the doctor who had to pump your stomach this afternoon. It was most unpleasant. I was worried my false hair might slip, but it didn't. All those things you've been doing, Edward. Strange that you can't remember them. Do you remember buying this gun this afternoon?'

'I—'

'You did, you know. Only an hour ago. You had to sign for it. Had to show your driver's license, too.'

'How did you get my driver's license?'

'I didn't. I created it.' The man laughed softly. 'It wouldn't fool a policeman, but no policeman saw it. It fooled the clerk though. Not the suicidal type? All those people will swear you are, Edward.'

'What about my friends? The people at the office?'

'They'll all help. They'll start to remember your moods. I'm sure you've been acting very shocked and unhappy about her death. You had to play the part, didn't you? You should never have killed her, Edward. I loved her, even if you didn't. You should have let her go, Edward.'

Wright was shaking with fear. 'You said you weren't going to murder me. You were going to leave me with the gun—'

'Don't believe everything you hear,' the man said, and, very quickly, he pushed the gun into Wright's mouth and shot him. Afterwards, he arranged things neatly, wiped his own fingerprints from the gun and put Wright's fingerprints on it. He left the note on top of the desk, put the psychiatrist's business card into Wright's wallet, and the receipt for the gun into Wright's pocket.

'You shouldn't have killed her,' he said to Wright's dead body. Then, smiling privately, he went out of the back door and walked off into the night.

Death on Christmas Eve
STANLEY ELLIN

As a child I had been impressed by the Boerum House. It was fairly new then, and shiny with new paint – a huge Victorian building. Standing in front of it this early Christmas Eve, however, I could find no echo of that youthful impression. It was all a depressing gray now, and the curtains behind the windows were drawn completely so that the house seemed to present blindly staring eyes to the passerby.

When I knocked my stick sharply on the door, Celia opened it. 'There is a doorbell,' she said.

She was still wearing the long unfashionable and badly wrinkled black dress which must have been her mother's, and she looked more than ever like old Katrin had in her later years: the thin bony body, the tight thin line of her lips, the colorless hair pulled back hard enough to remove every wrinkle from her forehead. She reminded me of a steel trap ready to shut down on anyone who touched her incautiously.

I said, 'I am aware that the doorbell is not connected, Celia,' and walked past her into the hall. She banged the door shut, and instantly we were in half-darkness.

I put out my hand for the light switch, but Celia said sharply, 'This is no time for lights! There's been a death in this house, you know that.'

'I have good reason to know,' I said, 'but your manner now does not impress me.'

11

'She was my brother's wife, and very dear to me.'

I moved towards her and rested my stick on her shoulder. 'Celia,' I said, 'as your family's lawyer, let me give you a word of advice. The inquest is over, and you've been cleared. But nobody believed you then, and nobody ever will. Remember that.'

She pulled away. 'Is that what you came to tell me?'

'I came because I knew your brother would want to see me today. I suggest you keep away while I talk to him.'

'Keep away from him yourself!' she cried. 'He was at the inquest and saw them clear my name. In a little while he'll forget the terrible things he thinks about me. Keep away from him so that he can forget.'

I started walking cautiously up the dark stairs, but she followed me. 'I prayed,' she said, 'and was told that life is too short for hatred. So when he comes to me, I'll forgive him.'

I reached the top of the stairs and almost fell over something. I swore, then said, 'If you're not going to use lights, you should at least keep the way clear. Why don't you get these things out of here?'

'They are poor Jessie's things,' she said. 'Ready for throwing out. It hurts Charlie to see anything of hers. I knew it would be best to throw them out.' Alarm came into her voice. 'But you won't tell him, will you?'

I went into Charlie's room and closed the door behind me. The curtains were drawn, but the ceiling light showed me that he was lying on his bed with an arm over his eyes. Slowly, he stood up and looked at me.

'Well,' he said at last, nodding towards the door, 'she didn't give you any light on the way up, did she?'

'No,' I said, 'but I know the way.'

'She gets around better in the dark than I do in the light. She'd rather have it that way, too. Otherwise she might look into a mirror and be frightened of what she saw.' He gave a short laugh. 'All you hear from her now is how she loved Jessie, and how sorry she is. Maybe she thinks if she says it often enough, people will believe it.'

I dropped my hat and stick on the bed and put my overcoat beside them. Then I took out a cigarette and waited until he found a match to light it for me. His hand shook violently. Charlie was five years younger than Celia, but seeing him then I thought he looked ten years older. His hair was so fair that it was difficult to see whether or not he was going gray. He had not shaved for several days, and there were huge blue-black bags under his eyes. He stared at me, pulling uncertainly at his mustache.

'You know why I wanted to see you,' he said.

'I can imagine,' I said, 'but I'd rather you told me.'

'It's Celia,' he said. 'I want her to get what she deserves. Not prison. I want the law to take her and kill her, and I want to be there to watch it.'

'You were at the inquest, Charlie,' I said. 'You saw what happened. Celia's cleared and, unless more evidence can be produced, she stays cleared.'

'What more evidence does anyone need! They were arguing violently at the top of the stairs. Celia threw Jessie down to the bottom and killed her. That's murder, isn't it?'

I was tired, and sat down in the old leather armchair. 'There were no witnesses,' I said.

'I heard Jessie scream and I heard her fall,' he said, 'and when

I ran out and found her there, I heard Celia bang her door shut. She pushed Jessie!'

'But you didn't *see* anything. And Celia says she wasn't there. As you weren't an eyewitness, you can't make a murder out of what might have been an accident.'

He slowly shook his head. 'You don't really believe that,' he said. 'Because if you do, you can get out now and never come near me again.'

'It doesn't matter what I believe. I'm telling you the legal position. What about motive? What did Celia have to gain from Jessie's death? There's no money or property involved.'

Charlie sat down on the edge of his bed. 'No,' he whispered, 'there's no money or property in it. It's me. First, it was the old lady with her heart trouble whenever I tried to do anything for myself. Then when she died and I thought I was free, it was Celia. She never had a husband or a baby – but she had me!'

'She's your sister, Charlie. She loves you.'

He laughed unpleasantly. 'And she can't let me go. When I think back now, I still can't understand how she did it. She would look at me in a certain way and all the strength would go out of me. And it was like that until I met Jessie . . . I remember the day I brought Jessie home, and told Celia we were married. There was a look in her eye – the same look that must have been there when she pushed Jessie down those stairs.'

I said, 'But you admitted at the inquest that you never saw her threaten or do anything to hurt Jessie.'

'Of course I never *saw*! But Jessie would go around sick to her heart every day without saying a word, and would cry in bed every night and not tell me why. I knew what was going on. I talked to her and I talked to Celia, and both of them just shook their heads. But when I saw Jessie lying there, it didn't surprise me at all.'

'I don't think it surprised anyone who knows Celia,' I said, 'but that isn't evidence.'

He beat his hand against his knee. 'What can I do? That's what I need you to tell me. All my life I've never done anything because of her. And that's what she expects now – that I won't do anything, and that she'll get away with it.' He stood up and stared at the door, then at me. 'But I can do something,' he whispered. 'Do you know what?'

I stood up facing him and shook my head. 'Whatever you're thinking, put it out of your mind,' I said.

'Don't confuse me,' he said. 'You know you can get away with murder if you're as clever as Celia. Don't you think I'm as clever as Celia?'

I held his shoulders. 'Don't talk like that, Charlie!'

He pulled away. His eyes were bright and his teeth showed behind his lips. 'What should I do?' he cried. 'Forget everything now Jessie is dead and buried? Sit here until Celia gets tired of being afraid of me and kills me too?'

'You haven't been out of this house since the inquest,' I said. 'It's about time you went out.'

'And have everybody laugh at me!' he said.

'Al Sharp said that some of your friends would be at his bar tonight, and he'd like to see you there,' I said. 'That's my advice – for whatever it's worth.'

'It's not worth anything,' said Celia. The door had opened and she stood there, her eyes narrowed against the light in the room. Charlie turned towards her.

'I told you never to come into this room!' he said.

'Did you have your ear at the door
long enough to hear everything I said?'

Her face remained calm. 'I'm not *in* it. I came to tell you that
your dinner is ready.'

He took a threatening step towards her. 'Did you have your
ear at the door long enough to hear everything I said?' he asked.
'Or shall I repeat it for you?'

'I heard an invitation to go *drinking* while this house is still
in mourning,' she said, 'and I object to that.'

He looked at her, amazed. 'Celia, tell me you don't mean that! Only the blackest hypocrite alive or someone mad could say what you've just said, and mean it.'

'Mad!' she cried. '*You* dare use that word? Locked in your room, talking to yourself.' She turned to me suddenly. 'You've talked to him. Is it possible—?'

'He's as sane as you, Celia,' I said.

'Then he knows he shouldn't drink in bars at a time like this. How could you ask him to do it?'

'If you weren't preparing to throw out Jessie's things, Celia,' I said, 'I would take that question seriously.' It was a dangerous thing to say, and I immediately regretted it. Before I could move, Charlie was past me and was holding Celia's arms tightly.

'Did you dare go into her room?' he shouted, shaking her. And getting an immediate answer from her face, he dropped her arms as if they were red hot, and stood there with his head down. 'Where are her things?'

'By the stairs, Charlie. Everything is there.'

He walked out of the room, and Celia turned to look at me. There was such terrible hatred in her face that I desperately wanted to get out of that house. I took my things from the bed, but she stood in front of the door.

'Do you see what you've done?' she said in a rough whisper. 'Now I will have to pack them all again – just because of you. You old fool! It should have been you with her when I—'

I dropped my stick sharply on her shoulder. 'As your lawyer, Celia,' I said, 'I advise you to speak only during your sleep, when you can't be made responsible for what you say.'

She said no more, but I made sure she stayed safely in front of me until I was out in the street again.

It was only a few minutes walk to Al Sharp's bar, and I was grateful for the clear winter air in my face. Al was alone behind the bar, polishing glasses.

'Merry Christmas,' he said, and put a comfortable-looking bottle and two glasses on the bar. 'I was expecting you.' Al poured two drinks. We drank, and he leaned across the bar. 'Just come from there?'

'Yes,' I said.

'See Charlie?'

'And Celia,' I said.

'I've seen her too when she goes by to do some shopping,' he said. 'Runs along with her head down, as if she's being chased by something. And I guess she is.'

'I guess she is, too,' I said.

'Did you tell Charlie I'd like to see him some time?'

'Yes,' I said. 'I told him.'

'What did he say?'

'Nothing. Celia said it was wrong for him to come here while he was in mourning.'

Al whistled softly, and moved a finger in circles at his forehead in a silent, 'crazy!'. 'Tell me,' he said, 'do you think it's safe for them to be alone together? The way things are, the way Charlie feels, there could be more trouble there.'

'It looked like that for a while tonight,' I said. 'But then it calmed down.'

'Until the next time,' said Al.

'I'll be there,' I said.

Al looked at me and shook his head. 'Nothing changes in that house,' he said. 'That's how you can work out all the answers. That's how I knew you'd be standing here now talking to me about it.'

I could still smell the dampness of the house, and I knew it would take days to get it out of my clothes.

'This is one day I'd like to take out of the year permanently,' I said.

'And leave them alone with their problems,' agreed Al.

'They're not alone,' I said. 'Jessie is with them. Jessie will always be with them until that house and everything in it is gone.'

Al frowned. 'It's the strangest thing that ever happened in this town. The house all black, her running through the streets like something hunted, him lying there in that room with only the walls to look at, for – how long? When was it Jessie had that fall?'

By moving my eyes a little I could see my face in the mirror behind Al: red, deeply lined, a little amazed. 'Twenty years,' I heard myself saying. 'Just twenty years ago tonight.'

The Heroine
PATRICIA HIGHSMITH

The girl was so sure she would get the job that she had come to Westchester with her suitcase. She sat in the living room of the Christiansens' house, looking, in her plain blue coat and hat, even younger than her twenty-one years.

'Have you worked as a governess before?' Mr Christiansen asked. He sat beside his wife on the sofa. 'Any references, I mean?'

'I was a maid at Mr Dwight Howell's home in New York for the last seven months.' Lucille looked at him with suddenly wide gray eyes. 'I could get a reference from there if you like . . . But when I saw your advertisement this morning, I didn't want to wait. I've always wanted a place where there are children.'

Mrs Christiansen smiled at the girl's enthusiasm, and said, 'We might phone them, of course . . . What do you say, Ronald? You wanted someone who really liked children . . .'

And fifteen minutes later Lucille Smith was standing in her room in the servants' house, at the back of the big house, putting on her new white uniform.

'You're starting again, Lucille,' she told herself in the mirror. 'You're going to forget everything that happened before.'

But her eyes grew too wide again, as though to deny her words. They looked like her mother's when they opened like that, and her mother was part of what she must forget.

There were only a few things to remember. A few silly habits, like burning bits of paper in ashtrays, forgetting time sometimes – little things that many people did, but that she must remember not to do. With practice she would remember, because she was just like other people (hadn't the psychiatrist told her so?).

She looked out at the garden and lawn that lay between the servants' house and the big house. The garden was longer than it was wide, and there was a fountain in the center. It was a beautiful garden! And trees so high and close together that Lucille could not see through them, and did not have to admit or believe that there was another house somewhere beyond . . . The Howell house in New York, tall and heavily ornamented, looking like an old wedding cake in a row of other old wedding cakes.

The Christiansen house was friendly, and alive! There were children in it! Thank God for the children. But she had not even met them yet.

She hurried downstairs and went across to the big house. What had the Christiansens agreed to pay her? She could not remember and did not care. She would have worked for nothing just to live in such a place.

Mrs Christiansen took her upstairs to the nursery where the children lay on the floor among colored pencils and picture books.

'Nicky, Heloise, this is your new nurse,' their mother said. 'Her name is Lucille.'

The little boy stood up and said, 'How do you do.'

'And Heloise,' Mrs Christiansen said, leading the second child, who was smaller, to Lucille.

Heloise stared and said, 'How do you do.'

'Nicky is nine, and Heloise six.'

Lucille could not take her eyes from them. They were the perfect children of her perfect house. They looked up at her with eyes that were curious, trusting, loving.

Mrs Christiansen smoothed the little girl's hair with a loving gentleness that fascinated Lucille. 'It's just about time for their lunch,' she said. 'You'll have your meals up here, Lucille. Lisabeth will be up with the lunch in a few minutes.' She paused at the door. 'You aren't nervous about anything, are you, Lucille?'

'Oh, no, madam.'

'Well, you mustn't be.' She seemed about to say something else, but only smiled and went out.

Lucille stared after her, wondering what that something else might have been.

'You're a lot prettier than Catherine,' Nicky told her. 'Catherine was our nurse before. She went back to Scotland. We didn't like Catherine.'

'No,' said Heloise. 'We didn't like Catherine.'

Nicky stared at his sister. 'You shouldn't say that. That's what I said!'

Lucille laughed. Then Nicky and Heloise laughed too.

A maid entered with lunch and put it on the table in the center of the room. 'I'm Lisabeth Jenkins, miss,' she said shyly.

'My name's Lucille Smith,' the girl said.

'If you need anything, just shout,' said the maid.

There were three omelets and some tomato soup. Lucille's coffee was in a silver pot, and the children had two large glasses of milk.

It was wonderful to be with these children. She had always been clumsy at the Howell house, but here it would not matter if she dropped a plate or a spoon. The children would only laugh.

Lucille drank some of her coffee, but the cup slipped and she spilled some of the coffee on the cloth.

'Piggy!' laughed Heloise.

'Heloise!' said Nicky, and went to fetch some paper towels from the bathroom.

They cleaned up together.

'Dad always gives us a little of his coffee,' said Nicky, as he sat down again.

Lucille had been wondering if the children would mention her spilling the coffee to their mother. She sensed that Nicky was offering her a bribe. 'Does he?' she asked.

'He pours a little in our milk,' Nicky went on.

'Like this?' Lucille poured a bit into each glass.

The children gasped with pleasure. 'Yes!'

'Catherine wouldn't give us any coffee, would she, Heloise?' said Nicky.

'Not her!' Heloise took a long, delicious drink.

A happy feeling rose inside Lucille. The children liked her, there was no doubt of that.

She remembered going to public parks in the city, during the three years she had worked as a maid in different houses, just to sit and watch the children play. But they had usually been dirty and had used bad language. Once she had seen a mother hit her own child across the face. Lucille remembered how she had run away in pain and horror.

'Why do you have such big eyes?' Heloise demanded.

Lucille jumped. 'My mother had big eyes, too,' she said deliberately, as if confessing.

Her mother had been dead three weeks now, but it seemed

much longer. That was because she was forgetting all the hope of the last three years as she had waited for her mother to recover. But recover to what? The illness was something separate, something which had killed her mother. It had been stupid to hope for her mother to become sane, which she had never been. Even the doctors had told her that. And they had told her other things, about herself. Good, encouraging things; that she was as sane as her father had been.

'You haven't finished eating,' said Nicky.

'I wasn't very hungry,' said Lucille.

'We could go out to the sand-box now,' he suggested. 'I want you to see our castle.'

The sand-box was in the back corner of the house. Lucille sat on the wooden edge of the box and watched while the children built their sand-castle.

'I'm the young queen, and I'm a prisoner in the castle!' Heloise shouted.

'Yes, and I'll rescue her, Lucille!' shouted Nicky.

When the castle was finished, Nicky put six small colored stones just inside. 'These are the good soldiers,' he said. 'They're prisoners in the castle, too.' Heloise got more small stones from the garden. She was to be the castle army as well as the queen.

As the game continued, Lucille found herself wishing for something really dangerous to happen to Heloise, so that she could prove her great courage and loyalty. She would be seriously wounded herself, perhaps with a bullet or a knife, but she would beat off the attacker. Then the Christiansens would love her and keep her with them always.

'O-o-ow!'

It was Heloise. Nicky had pushed one of her fingers against

the edge of the box as they struggled to get the same small stone.

Lucille was alarmed at the sight of the blood, and was wildly afraid that Lisabeth or Mrs Christiansen might see it. She took Heloise to the bathroom next to the nursery, and gently washed the finger. It was only a small scratch, and Heloise soon stopped her tears.

'Look, it's only a little scratch!' Lucille said, but it was said to calm the children. To Lucille it was not a little scratch. It was a terrible disaster which she had failed to prevent. And on her first afternoon!

Heloise smiled. 'Don't punish Nicky. He didn't mean to do it.' And she ran from the bathroom and jumped on to her bed. 'We have to have our afternoon sleep now,' she told Lucille. 'Goodbye.'

'Goodbye,' Lucille answered, and tried to smile.

She went down to get Nicky, and when they came back up Mrs Christiansen was at the nursery door.

Lucille's face went white. 'I don't think it's bad, madam. It – it's a scratch from the sand-box.'

'Heloise's finger? Oh, don't worry, my dear. They're always getting little scratches. Nicky, dear, you must learn to be more gentle. Look how you frightened Lucille!' She laughed and ruffled his hair.

While the children slept, Lucille looked at one of their story books. The hospital doctor had encouraged her reading, she remembered, and had told her to go to the cinema, too. 'Be with normal people and forget all about your mother's difficulties...'

And the psychiatrist had said, 'There's no reason why you should not be as normal as your father was. Get a job outside the city – relax, enjoy life. Forget even the house your family lived in. After a year . . .'

That, too, was three weeks ago, just after her mother had died. And what the doctor had said was true. In this house, where there was peace and love, beauty and children, she would forget for ever her mother's face.

With a little gasp of joy, she pressed her face into the pages of the story book, her eyes half closed. Slowly she rocked backwards and forwards in the chair, conscious of nothing but her own happiness.

'What are you doing?' Nicky asked, politely curious.

Lucille brought the book down from her face. She smiled like a happy but guilty child. 'Reading!' she laughed.

Nicky laughed too. 'You read very close!'

'Ye-es,' said Heloise, who had also sat up.

Nicky came over and looked at the book. 'We get up at three o'clock. Would you read to us now? Catherine always read to us until dinner.'

Lucille sat down on the floor so they could see the pictures as she read. She read for two hours, and the time slipped by. Just after five, Lisabeth brought their dinner, and when the meal was over Nicky and Heloise demanded more reading until bedtime. Lucille gladly began another book, but Lisabeth came to say that it was time for the children's bath, and that Mrs Christiansen would be up to say good night in a little while.

When the children were in bed, Lucille went downstairs with Mrs Christiansen.

'Is everything all right, Lucille?'

'Yes, madam. Except . . . can I come up once in the night to see that the children are all right?'

'That's a very kind thought, Lucille, but it really isn't necessary.'

Lucille was silent.

'I'm afraid the evenings are going to seem long to you. If you ever want to go to the cinema in town, Alfred, that's the chauffeur, will be glad to take you in the car.'

'Thank you, madam.'

'Then good night, Lucille.'

Lucille went out the back way and across the garden. When she opened her door, she wished it was the nursery door; that it was morning and time to begin another day.

How good, she thought as she turned out the light, to feel pleasantly tired (although it was only nine o'clock) instead of being unable to sleep because of thinking about her mother or worrying about herself. She remembered one day not so long ago when for fifteen minutes she had been unable to think of her name. She had run in fear to the doctor.

That was past! She might even ask Alfred to buy her some cigarettes – a luxury she had denied herself for months.

The second day was like the first – except that there was no scratched hand – and so was the third and the fourth. The only thing that changed was Lucille's love for the family. A love which grew greater each day.

Saturday evening she found an envelope addressed to herself at the servants' house. Inside was $20.

It meant nothing to her. To use it she would have to go to the shops where other people were. What use had she for money if she was never to leave the Christiansen home? In a year's time she would have $1040, and in two years $2080. Eventually she would have as much as the Christiansens, and that would not be right.

Would they think it was very strange if she asked to work for nothing? Or for $10 perhaps?

She went to see Mrs Christiansen the next morning.

'It's about my pay, madam,' she said. 'It's too much for me.'

Mrs Christiansen looked surprised. 'You *are* a funny girl, Lucille! You want to be with the children day and night. You're always talking about doing something "important" for us. And now your pay is too much!' She laughed. 'You're certainly different, Lucille!'

Lucille was listening closely. 'How do you mean different, madam?'

'I've just told you, my dear. And I refuse to pay you less because that would be treating you badly. In fact, if you ever want more—'

'Oh, no, madam! But I wish there was something more I could do for you, and the children. Something bigger—'

'Nonsense, Lucille,' Mrs Christiansen interrupted. 'Mr Christiansen and I are both very pleased with you.'

'Thank you, madam.'

Lucille went back to the nursery where the children were playing. Mrs Christiansen did not understand. If she could just explain about her mother, and her fear of herself for so many months, how she had never dared take even a cigarette, and how just being with the family in this beautiful house had made her well again . . .

That night she sat in her room with the light on until after twelve o'clock. She had her cigarettes now, and allowed herself just three in the evening, but even these were enough to relax her mind, to make her dream of being a heroine. And when the

She tore the $20 bill into bits and added these to the fire.

three cigarettes were smoked and she would have liked another, she put them in her top drawer so that they could not tempt her.

She noticed the $20 bill the Christiansens had given her. She took a match and lit it, and put the burning end down against the side of her ashtray. Slowly she lit the rest of the matches, one after another, and made a tiny, well controlled fire. When all the matches were burnt, she tore the $20 bill into bits and added these to the fire.

Mrs Christiansen did not understand, but if she saw *this*, she might. But *this* was not enough. Just loyal service was not enough either. Anyone would give that, for money. She was different. Mrs Christiansen had said that. Lucille remembered what else Mrs Christiansen had said: 'Mr Christiansen and I are both very pleased with you.' Lucille smiled at the memory. She felt wonderfully strong and happy. Only one thing was lacking in her happiness. She had to prove herself in a crisis.

She moved nervously around the room.

If only there were a flood . . . She imagined the water coming higher and higher around the house, until it almost rushed into the nursery. She would rescue the children and swim with them to safety.

Or if there were an earthquake . . . She would rush in among falling walls and pull the children out. Perhaps she would go back for some small thing – one of Nicky's toys – and be killed! *Then* the Christiansens would know how much she loved them.

Or if there were a fire . . . Fires were common things. There might be a terrible fire just from the gasoline that was in the garage . . .

She went downstairs, through the door that opened into the garage. The gasoline tank was three feet high and completely full. Despite its weight, she got it out of the garage and rolled it across the garden, making no noise on the grass. The windows were dark, but even if there had been lights Lucille would not have stopped. Nor if Mr Christiansen himself had been standing by the fountain, because probably she would not have seen him.

She poured some gasoline on a corner of the house, rolled the tank further, and poured some more. She went on like this until she reached the far corner. Then she lit a match and walked back the way she had come, touching it against the wet places. Without looking back, she went to stand by the door of the servants' house to watch.

At first the flames were pale and eager, then they became yellow with bits of red. Lucille began to relax. She would let the flames grow tall, even to the nursery window, before she rushed in, so that the danger would be at its highest.

A smile came to her mouth, and her face was bright in the light of the fire. Anyone seeing her there would certainly have thought her a beautiful young woman.

She had lit the fire at five places, and now it was creeping up the house like the fingers of a hand, warm and gentle. Lucille smiled, but made herself wait.

Suddenly the gasoline tank, having grown too warm, exploded with a sound like a huge gun and lit up the whole garden for an instant.

As though this was the sign for which she had been waiting, Lucille went confidently forward.

Ride the Lightning

JOHN LUTZ

A sheet of rain moved across Placid Cove Trailer Park.
Lightning made a complicated pattern in the night sky.
Nudger held his umbrella against the wind as he walked, and
pulled a piece of paper from his pocket to check the address of
the trailer he was trying to find. Finally, he found Number 307
and knocked on its metal door.

'I'm Nudger,' he said, when the door opened.

The woman in the doorway stared at him. Rain blew in,
making wet marks on her pale blue dress and ruffling her blond
hair. She was tall but very thin. She looked at first to be about
twelve years old, but a second glance showed her to be in her
middle twenties. She had blue eyes, a large mouth, and top teeth
that rested on her bottom lip when she wasn't talking.

'This rain's terrible,' she said at last, as if seeing beyond
Nudger for the first time.

'It is,' Nudger agreed. 'And it's raining on me.'

Her whole body gave a quick, nervous movement as she
smiled to apologize. 'I'm Holly Ann Adams, Mr Nudger. And
yes, you are getting wet. Come in.'

The trailer was small, and crowded with cheap furniture.
Shouts and laughter came from a program on a small black-
and-white TV, which was on a tiny table near a worn-out sofa.
The air smelled of food which had been fried too long.

Holly Ann moved a pile of magazines from a chair. Nudger folded his umbrella and sat down. She started to speak, then there was that same nervous movement again, as if she'd remembered something, and she walked over and switched off the TV.

'Are you a real private detective?' she said.

'I am,' Nudger said. 'Did someone recommend me to you, Miss Adams?'

'I got your name out of the phone book. And if you're going to work for me, it can be Holly Ann without the Adams.'

'Except on the check,' Nudger said.

She smiled a wicked twelve-year-old's smile. 'Oh, sure, don't worry about that. I already wrote you a check, I just have to fill in the amount. That's if you agree to take the job. You might not.'

'Why not?'

'It's to do with my fiancé, Curtis Colt.'

For a few seconds Nudger listened to the rain crashing on the roof, then he said, 'The Curtis Colt who's going to be executed next week?'

'That's the one. But he didn't kill that liquor store woman, and that's a fact. It's not right that he should have to ride the lightning.'

'Ride the lightning?'

'That's what prisoners call dying in the electric chair. Curtis doesn't belong in it, and I can prove it.'

'It's a little late for that kind of talk,' Nudger said. 'Or did you give evidence for Curtis in court?'

'No, I couldn't. All those lawyers and the judge and jury don't even know about me. Curtis didn't want them to know, so he never told them.'

'Tell me about Curtis Colt,' Nudger said. 'Give me the details.'

'Well, they say Curtis was inside the liquor store, robbing it. He and his partner had robbed three other places that night, but they were gas stations. The old man who owned the store came out of the back room and saw his wife with her hands up, and Curtis pointing a gun at her. He went crazy and ran at Curtis, and Curtis had to shoot him. Then the woman went mad and ran at Curtis, and Curtis shot her. She died. The old man will live, but he can't talk or even feed himself.'

Nudger remembered now. Curtis Colt had been found guilty of murder. And because the law had now decided to stop using poison gas to execute people, he would be the first killer to die in the electric chair for more than twenty-five years.

'They're going to shoot Curtis full of electricity next Saturday, Mr Nudger,' Holly Ann said. Her wide blue eyes stared at Nudger. 'I have bad dreams about it. Then I lie awake, thinking. I've just got to do whatever's left to try and help Curtis.'

'They never caught Curtis's partner, the driver who drove away and left him in that gas station, did they?' Nudger asked.

'No. And Curtis would never say who the driver was.'

'But you know who was driving the car.'

'Yes. And he told me that he and Curtis were miles away from that liquor store when it was robbed. When he saw the police come into that gas station where Curtis was buying cigarettes, he got out of there fast. The cops didn't even get the car's license number.'

Nudger rubbed a hand across his chin and watched Holly Ann. 'The jury thought Curtis shot the old man and the woman deliberately, in cold blood.'

'That's not true! Not according to—' She stopped herself before saying the man's name.

'Curtis's friend,' Nudger finished.

'That's right. And he ought to know,' she said.

'None of this means anything unless the driver comes forward and says he was somewhere else with Curtis when the liquor store was robbed,' Nudger said.

Holly Ann nodded. 'I know. But he won't. He can't. That's why I need you. The witnesses who say they saw Curtis at the liquor store are wrong. I want you to find a way to convince them of that.'

'Four people, two of them customers in the store, picked Curtis out of a police line-up,' Nudger reminded her.

'So what? Eye witnesses often make mistakes.'

Nudger had to admit that they did.

'Talk to them,' she said. 'Find out *why* they think Curtis was the killer. Show them how they might be wrong, and get them to change their stories.'

'Even if all the witnesses change their stories, Curtis might not get a new trial,' Nudger said.

'Perhaps not, but the law wouldn't kill him if enough witnesses said they were wrong. Then, maybe, eventually, he'd get another trial and get out of prison.'

He had to admire her. She was prepared to believe the impossible.

'So will you help me, Mr Nudger?'

'Sure. It sounds easy.'

'Why should I worry about it any more?' Randy Gantner asked Nudger. He didn't mind talking, because he could have a rest

'So will you help me, Mr Nudger?'

from his construction job on the new road. 'Colt's been found guilty and he's going to the electric chair, isn't he?'

Holly Ann had given Nudger a photograph of Curtis Colt. Now Nudger held it for Gantner to see. 'This is a picture you never saw in court. Just look at it closely and tell me again if you're sure the man you saw in the liquor store was Colt.'

'I'd be a fool to change my story now,' Gantner said.

'You'd be a murderer if you really weren't sure.'

Gantner sighed and looked at the photograph. 'It's Colt. He

shot the man and woman while I was standing at the back of the store. If he'd known me and Sanders were there, he'd have probably shot us, too.'

'You're positive it's the same man?'

Gantner began to look annoyed. 'I said it to the police and jury, Nudger. Colt killed the old lady.'

'Did you actually see the shots fired?'

'No. We were at the back of the store looking for some cheap whisky when we heard the shots. We saw Colt run out to the car – a black or dark green Ford. Colt fired another shot as it drove away.'

'Did you see the driver?'

'I saw a thin man with curly black hair and a mustache. And that's what I told the cops.'

The other witnesses also identified Curtis Colt from the photograph. The last witness was an elderly woman named Iris Langerneckert who had seen Colt run out of the store and into the car. Like Gantner, she said the driver was a thin man with curly black hair and a mustache, but then she added, 'Like Curtis Colt's hair and mustache.'

Nudger looked again at the photograph. Curtis Colt was thin, with a thick mustache and curly black hair. Was it possible that the car driver had been Curtis Colt himself, and that it was his partner who had shot the shopkeeper? Nudger found that hard to believe.

He decided he needed more information about the robbery and about Curtis Colt, so he drove east towards the Third District police station.

Ten years ago, Police Lieutenant Jack Hammersmith had been Nudger's partner in a two-man police car, but now he looked much older and heavier than the handsome cop Nudger had once worked with.

'Sit down, Nudge,' Hammersmith invited.

'I need some help,' Nudger said.

'Sure,' Hammersmith said.

'I need to know more about Curtis Colt.'

Hammersmith lit a cigar. 'Colt? The man who's going to ride the lightning?'

'That's the second time in the past few days I've heard that expression. The first time was from Colt's fiancée. She thinks he's innocent.'

'Fiancées think like that. Are you working for her?'

Nudger nodded.

'I was in charge of that murder investigation,' said Hammersmith. 'Colt's guilty, Nudge.'

'The description of the car driver is a lot like Colt's. Maybe he did the shooting and Colt was the driver.'

'Colt's lawyer suggested that. The jury didn't believe it. Neither do I. The man's guilty, Nudge.'

'Can I see the papers for the Colt case?'

Hammersmith finished his cigar. 'Why didn't this fiancée come to the trial and speak for Colt? She could have lied and said he was with her that night.'

'Colt didn't want her to have to give evidence.'

'So what makes her think Colt is innocent?'

'She knows he was somewhere else that night.'

'But not with her,' Hammersmith said.

'No,' Nudger said.

Hammersmith picked up the phone and asked for the Colt papers to be brought to him. Nudger looked at them, but didn't find out much that he didn't already know. Fifteen minutes after the robbery, officers from a two-man police car, acting on a radio description of the gunman, approached Curtis Colt inside a gas station where he was buying cigarettes. A car had been parked nearby and it drove away fast when the police car arrived. The officers got only a quick look at it – a dark green Ford with a license plate that might start with the letter 'L'.

Colt went with the policemen to the Third District police station, and later that night the four eyewitnesses had picked him out of a line-up. Their description of the car matched the one driving away from the gas station. The money from the robbery, and several gas station robberies, wasn't on Colt, but was probably in the car.

'What about the gun?' Nudger asked.

'Colt wasn't carrying a gun when we arrested him.'

'Seems odd,' Nudger said.

'Not really. He was buying cigarettes. He left the gun in the car.'

Nudger put the papers back on Hammersmith's desk. 'I'll let you know if I learn anything interesting.'

'It's over, Nudge,' Hammersmith said. 'I don't see how even the fiancée can doubt Colt's guilt.'

'She has bad dreams about Colt dying in the electric chair,' Nudger said.

'Colt probably has bad dreams, too,' Hammersmith said. 'But he deserves his.'

'None of the witnesses are in any doubt about identifying Curtis Colt as the killer,' Nudger said to Holly Ann in her trailer the next day.

'They know what's going to happen to Curtis,' she said. 'They don't want to live knowing they might have made a mistake and killed an innocent man, so they've convinced themselves it was Curtis they saw.' She looked at him for a moment or two, then went on, 'I see you need to be convinced of Curtis's innocence. Come here tonight at eight, Mr Nudger, and I'll convince you.'

'How?'

'I can't tell you. You'll understand why tonight.'

'Why do we have to wait until tonight?'

'Oh, you'll see.'

Nudger felt as if they were playing a children's guessing game while Curtis Colt waited to go to the electric chair. He had never seen an execution. He'd heard it took longer than most people thought for the prisoner to die.

At eight o'clock that evening, Nudger was sitting at the tiny table in Holly Ann's kitchen. Opposite him was a thin, nervous man in his late twenties, dressed in a shirt with long sleeves despite the heat, and wearing sunglasses. Holly Ann introduced him as 'Len, but that's not his real name,' and said he was Colt's partner and the driver of the car on the night of the murder.

'But me and Curtis weren't anywhere near the liquor store when those people got shot,' he said.

Nudger assumed the sunglasses were so that he couldn't identify Len if they ever went to court. Len had dark brown hair that fell to his shoulders, and when he moved his arm Nudger saw something blue and red on his wrist. A tattoo. Which explained the long-sleeved shirt.

'Your hair didn't grow that long in the three months since

the liquor store killing,' Nudger said, 'so that helps you. The witnesses say the driver had short curly hair, like Colt's, and a mustache.'

'I'll be honest with you,' Len said. 'Me and Curtis looked alike. So, to confuse any witnesses if we got caught, I used to put my hair up and wear a wig that looks like Curtis's hair. And I shaved off my mustache a month ago.'

'Can you prove you were the other side of the town at the time of the murder?' Nudger asked.

'No, but I'm telling the truth. I just want you to believe Curtis is innocent,' said Len, desperately. 'Because he is! And so am I!'

Nudger understood why Len was taking a risk coming here. If Colt was guilty of murder, Len was guilty of being at the liquor store with him. Once Colt was dead, there was always a chance that Len would be caught and sent to prison for life, or even be executed. It wasn't necessary to actually fire the gun to be found guilty of murder.

'Are you giving Holly Ann the money to pay me?' Nudger asked.

'Some of it, yes,' Len said. 'I gave her some of the money Curtis and I stole.'

Dirty money, Nudger thought. Dirty job. But if Curtis Colt was innocent . . .

'OK, I'll keep working on this.'

'Thanks,' Len said. 'Stay here with Holly Ann for ten minutes after I leave. I want to know I'm not being followed. It's not that I don't trust you, but I've got to be sure, you understand?'

'I understand. Go.'

Len went out and Nudger heard him running away.

'You know I have to tell the police about this conversation, don't you?' Nudger said to Holly Ann.

She nodded. 'That's why we arranged it this way.'

'They might want to talk to you.'

'It doesn't matter,' Holly Ann said. 'I don't know where Len is, or even his real name. He'll find out all he needs to know about Curtis from the newspapers.'

'I don't believe it,' Hammersmith said angrily, chewing on his cigar. Angrily because he did believe it a little bit, and didn't like to think it was possible he was sending an innocent man to his death. 'This Len character is just trying to keep himself away from a murder trial.'

'It could be like that,' Nudger admitted.

'It would help if you gave us a better description of Len,' Hammersmith said, still angry.

'I gave you what I could,' Nudger said. 'Are you going to question Holly Ann?'

'Sure, but it won't do any good. She's probably telling the truth and doesn't know how to find Len.'

'You could have her trailer watched.'

'Do you think Holly Ann and Len might be lovers?'

'No,' Nudger said.

'Then they'll probably never see each other again. Watching her trailer would be a waste of time.'

Nudger knew Hammersmith was right. He stood up.

'What are you going to do now?' Hammersmith asked.

'I'll talk to the witnesses again, and read the trial papers again. And I'd like to talk with Curtis Colt.'

'They don't allow visitors on Death Row, Nudge.'

'Will you try to arrange it?'

Hammersmith chewed thoughtfully on his cigar. 'I'll phone you and let you know,' he said eventually.

That day Nudger managed to talk again to all four witnesses. None of them changed their stories. Nudger reported this to Holly Ann at the restaurant where she worked as a waitress. Several customers that afternoon got tears with their baked potatoes.

Hammersmith phoned Nudger that evening.

'Colt won't talk to you,' he said. 'He won't talk to anyone.'

'Does he know I'm working for Holly Ann?'

'Yes. He wasn't pleased.'

Nudger swore.

'This isn't your fault, Nudge,' Hammersmith said.

'We've got one more day before he's executed,' Nudger said. 'I'm going to talk to those witnesses again.'

'You're wasting your time, Nudge.'

Hammersmith was right. Nothing Nudger did helped Curtis Colt at all. At eight o'clock Saturday morning, while Nudger was preparing breakfast in his apartment, Colt died in the electric chair without saying any last words.

Nudger heard the news on his kitchen radio.

That afternoon, he apologized to Holly Ann for not being able to stop her lover's execution. She was polite, and tried to be brave. The restaurant owner gave her the day off, and Nudger drove her home.

Nudger slept a total of four hours during the next two nights. On Monday he went to Curtis Colt's funeral. There were twelve people around the grave. Holly Ann looked like a child playing dress-up in black. They didn't exchange words, only glances.

Afterwards, Nudger watched her walk to a taxi. She never looked back.

That night Nudger realized what was bothering him, and for the first time since Colt's death, he slept well.

In the morning he began watching Holly Ann's trailer. At seven-thirty she came out dressed in her yellow waitress uniform and got into a taxi. Nudger followed in his Volkswagen as the taxi drove her the four miles to her job at the restaurant. At six that evening another taxi drove her home, making a short stop at a food store.

The same thing happened every day that week. Holly Ann had no visitors. The weather got warmer, and Nudger sat in the hot Volkswagen and wondered if it was worth doing what he was doing.

The next Monday, after Holly Ann had left for work, Nudger got into the trailer. It took him more than an hour to find what he was searching for. It was a box hidden behind the bath. Inside were seven hundred dollars, and another object which Nudger wasn't surprised to see.

He closed the box and put it back.

He continued to watch Holly Ann, more confident now.

Two weeks after the funeral, when she left work one evening, she didn't go home. Instead her taxi drove east. Nudger followed through several narrow streets to a garage. The sign said: 'Cliff's Car Repairs'.

Nudger parked and waited until the taxi went by without a passenger. Ten minutes later, Holly drove by in a shiny red Ford. Its license plate began with an 'L'.

When Nudger reached Placid Cove Trailer Park, he saw the Ford next to Holly's trailer. He scratched the Ford's door with a key. Beneath the new red paint the car's color was dark green.

Holly Ann answered the door immediately when he knocked. She tried to smile when she saw it was him, but couldn't quite manage it. She looked ten years older, and was holding a glass with whisky in it.

'I know what happened,' Nudger told her.

Now she did smile, but only for a second. 'You don't know when to stop, Mr Nudger.'

He followed her into the trailer. It was hot inside. She offered him a drink, but he shook his head. She finished hers and poured herself another.

'Now what is it you know, Mr Nudger?' She didn't really want to know, but she had to hear it. Had to share it.

'The taxi fare to and from work must make a big hole in your wages. And you seem to go everywhere by taxi.'

'My car's been in the garage for repair,' she said.

'I guessed that, after I found the money and the wig.'

She drank some of her whisky. 'Wig?'

'In the box behind the bath,' Nudger said. 'You're thin, and with a dark curly wig and a false mustache, sitting in your car, you'd look enough like Curtis Colt to confuse any witnesses. It was a clever trick.'

Holly Ann looked amazed. 'Are you saying I was driving the car at the liquor store robbery?'

'Maybe. Then maybe you paid someone to be Len and convince me he was Colt's partner, and that they were far away from the liquor store when the old woman was murdered. After I found the wig, I talked to some of your neighbors. They told me that until recently you'd driven a green Ford.'

Holly Ann moved her tongue along her top teeth.

'So Curtis and Len used my car,' she said.

'I doubt if Len ever met Curtis. He's somebody you paid to sit there and lie to me,' Nudger said.

'If I was driving the car, Mr Nudger, and knew Curtis was guilty, why would I hire a private detective to try and find something wrong with the witnesses' stories?'

'That's what puzzled me at first,' Nudger said, 'until I realized you weren't interested in proving Curtis was innocent. What you were *really* worried about was Curtis talking in prison. You wanted to be sure those witnesses *wouldn't* change their stories. And you wanted the police to learn about not-his-right-name Len.'

'Why would I want that?' Holly Ann asked simply.

'Because you were Curtis Colt's partner in all his robberies. When you robbed the liquor store, he stayed in the car to drive. You fired the shot that killed the old woman. He fired the wild shot from the moving car. Colt kept quiet about it because he loved you. Now he's dead you can trust him forever, but I think you could have anyway. He loved you more than you loved him, and you'll have to live knowing that he didn't deserve to die.'

She looked into her glass, and didn't say anything for a long time. Then she said, 'I didn't want to shoot that old man, but he didn't leave me any choice. Then the old woman came up to me.' She looked up at Nudger and smiled. It was a smile he didn't like. 'God help me, Mr Nudger, I can't stop thinking about shooting that old woman.'

'You murdered her,' Nudger said, 'and you murdered Curtis Colt by letting him die for you.'

'You can't prove anything,' she said, still with the same frightening smile.

'You're right,' Nudger said, 'I can't. But Curtis Colt rode the lightning, and his bad dreams died with him. Yours will stay with you for years. I think you'll come to agree his way was easier.'

She sat very still. She didn't answer.

Nudger stood up and wiped his damp forehead with the back of his hand. He felt hot and dirty in the tiny trailer, and he wanted to get out.

He didn't say goodbye to Holly Ann when he walked out. She didn't say goodbye to him. The last thing Nudger heard as he left the trailer was the sound of the bottle clinking on the glass.

The Lipstick

MARY ROBERTS RINEHART

I walked home after the inquest. Mother had gone in the car, looking rather sick, as she had done since Elinor's death. Not that she had liked Elinor. My cousin Elinor Hammond had gone happily through life, as if she woke each morning wondering what would be the most fun that day; stretching her long lovely body between her silk sheets – how bitter mother was about those sheets! – and calling to poor tired old Fred in his dressing room.

'Let's have some people in for drinks, Fred.'

'Anything you say, my love.'

Anything Elinor said was all right with Fred. I remembered his face at the inquest – shocked and puzzled.

'You know of no reason why your – why Mrs Hammond should take her own life?'

'None at all.'

'Nothing about her health caused her anxiety?'

'Nothing. She always seemed to be in perfect health.'

'She was seeing Doctor Barclay.'

'She was tired,' he said unhappily.

But Elinor had either fallen or jumped from that tenth-floor window of Doctor Barclay's waiting room, and the coroner clearly believed she had jumped.

The doctor had not seen her that day. Only the nurse. 'There was no one else in the waiting room,' she told the coroner. 'The

49

doctor was with a patient. Mrs Hammond sat by the window, took off her hat, lit a cigarette and picked up a magazine. Then I went back to my office and didn't see her again until—'

She was a pretty little thing. She looked pale.

'What happened next?' said the coroner gently.

'I heard the other patient leave. She went out from the doctor's room. When he rang for the next patient, I went to get Mrs Hammond. She wasn't there. I saw her hat, but her bag was gone. Then . . .' She stopped and swallowed. 'Then I heard people shouting in the street and I looked out of the window.'

The coroner gave her a little time, then said, 'Would you say she was depressed that morning, Miss Comings?'

'I thought she seemed very cheerful,' she said.

'The window was open beside her?'

'Yes. I couldn't believe it . . .' She was crying by this time, and it was clear she had told all she knew.

Doctor Barclay, who had just come in, was called next. He was in his late thirties and quite good-looking. Knowing Elinor, I wondered. She had liked handsome men. Fred, who was not at all handsome, was the exception. Beside me, mother had also noticed the doctor's good looks. 'So that's it!' she said disapprovingly. 'Elinor had as much need for a psychiatrist as I need a third leg!'

The doctor had not seen Elinor at all that morning. When he rang and nobody came, he went to the waiting room where Miss Comings was looking out of the window. Suddenly, she began to scream. Fortunately a Mrs Thompson arrived at that time and went to help her.

Asked about Elinor's visits to him, he said, 'I have many patients who are nervous and anxious. Mrs Hammond had been like that for years.'

'That is all? She spoke of no particular trouble?'

He smiled faintly. 'We all have troubles. Some we imagine, some are real. But I would say that Mrs Hammond was an unusually normal person. I had recommended that she go away for a rest. I believe she meant to do so.'

His voice was cool and efficient. Fred, however, was watching him closely.

'You did not think that she intended suicide?'

'No. Not at any time.'

He would not speak about anything Elinor had imagined. His relationships with his patients, he said, were confidential. If he knew anything of value he would tell them, but he did not.

He sat down near us and the next witness was called. It was the Mrs Thompson who had looked after the nurse.

'I clean the doctor's apartment for him once a week,' she said. 'That day I needed a little money in advance, so I went to see him.'

She had not entered the office at once. She had looked in the waiting room and seen Elinor, and had waited in the hall where it was cool. She saw the last patient, a woman, leave the doctor's room and go down the stairs. A minute or so later she heard the nurse scream.

'She was looking out of the window screaming,' she said. 'The doctor ran in and we got her into a chair. Somebody had fallen out, she said, but didn't say who.'

Asked how long she had been in the hall, she thought about quarter of an hour. She was sure no other patient had entered during that time. She would have seen them.

'You found something belonging to Mrs Hammond, didn't

you? In the waiting room?'

'Yes, I found her bag.' The bag, it seemed, had been behind the radiator in front of the window. 'I thought it was a strange place for it, if she was going to – do what she did. I gave it to the police when they came.'

So Elinor, having put her hat on the table, had dropped her bag behind the radiator before she jumped. Somehow it didn't make sense to me.

The verdict was suicide. Nobody mentioned murder. After Mrs Thompson's evidence, it seemed impossible. Fred listened with dead eyes. His sister Margaret, sitting beside him, stood up. Doctor Barclay stared ahead of him, then he got up and went out.

I was angry as I walked home. I had always liked Elinor, even though mother said she took Fred away from me. But Fred never saw me after he first met her. He had loved her with a blind passion from the start.

The fools, I thought. Even if Elinor was in trouble, she would never have jumped out of a window. Somebody had killed her and had got away with it. Who hated her enough for that? A jealous wife? It was possible. She would play around with a woman's husband until she was tired of him. But she had not been doing that lately. She had been rather quiet. Of course, plenty of people had not liked her. She would ignore their feelings or laugh at them. She said what she had to say, and sometimes it wasn't pleasant. Even to Fred. But he had never got angry.

I thought about Fred sitting alone and it made me sad. His house was not far away, and after dinner that evening I went over. It was a large house, surrounded by its own grounds like ours, and a man was standing inside the gates, looking up at the house. He turned suddenly and looked at me. It was Doctor Barclay.

He didn't recognize me. I suppose he had not seen me at the inquest. He touched his hat and went out into the street, and a moment later I heard his car start. But if he had been in the house, Fred made no mention of it. He seemed relieved when he saw me.

'I thought you were the police again,' he said.

We went into the library. It looked as if it hadn't been cleaned for a month. Elinor's house had always looked like that; full of people and cigarette smoke and dirty drinks glasses. But at least it had looked alive. Now it didn't. So it was a surprise to see her bag on the table. Fred saw me looking at it.

'Police returned it today,' he said. 'Drink?'

'Thanks. Can I look inside it?'

He nodded. 'There's nothing in it that doesn't belong there. No note, if that's what you think.'

I opened the bag. It was full as usual: make-up, money, notebook, a handkerchief marked with lipstick, some pieces of dress material with a card saying 'Match shoes to these.' Fred watched me, his eyes red and tired. 'I told you. Nothing,' he said.

I searched the bag again, but could not find the thing that should have been there. I put it back on the table.

Fred was staring at a photograph of Elinor in a silver frame, on the desk. 'She was beautiful.'

'She was indeed,' I said honestly.

'Margaret thought she was a fool who spent too much money.' He glanced at the desk, piled high with unopened bills. 'Maybe she was, but what the hell did I care?'

He seemed to expect me to say something, so I said, 'You didn't have to buy her, Fred. She loved you dearly.'

He gave me a faint smile. 'I wasn't only her husband,' he said, 'I was her father, too. She told me everything. Why she had to go to that doctor . . .'

'Didn't you know she was going, Fred?'

'Not until I found a bill from him.' He talked on as if he was glad of an audience. He had made her happy. She went her own way sometimes, but she always came back to him. He thought the coroner's verdict was terribly wrong. 'She fell. She was always careless about heights.' And he had made no plans, except that Margaret was coming to stay until he closed the house.

And at that minute Margaret walked in.

I had never liked Margaret Hammond. She was a tall woman, older than Fred. She nodded to me.

'I decided to come tonight,' she said to Fred. 'I didn't like you being alone. And tomorrow I want to make a list of everything in the house. I'd like to have father's picture, Fred.'

He looked uncomfortable. There had been a long quarrel about old Joe Hammond's picture. Elinor had not cared about it, but because Margaret had wanted it she had kept it. I looked at Margaret. Perhaps she was the nearest thing to a real enemy Elinor had ever had.

She looked at the pile of bills on the desk. 'We'll have to find out how much money you owe.'

'I know how much money I owe,' he said.

He got up and they stared at each other, Fred with his back to the desk, as if even then he was protecting Elinor from Margaret. But as I left the house, I was fairly confident that Margaret would come downstairs later, when Fred was asleep, and go through those bills.

I was nearly home when I realized I was being followed. Feeling frightened, I stopped and turned. But it was only a girl. She spoke my name.

'Miss Baring? I saw you at the inquest and a newspaper man told me your name. You've been to the Hammonds', haven't you?'

'Yes. What about it?'

She was quite young and seemed nervous.

'Were you a friend of Mrs Hammond's?' she asked.

'She was my cousin. Why?'

She took a cigarette from her bag and lit it. 'Because I think she was pushed out of that window. I work in an office across the street, and I was looking out. I didn't know who she was, of course.'

'Do you mean you saw it happen?' I said, amazed.

'No. But I saw her at the window just before it happened, and she was using a lipstick. When I looked out again she was . . . on the pavement.' Her hand started to shake and she threw away the cigarette. 'I don't think a woman would use a lipstick just before she was going to do a thing like that, do you?'

'No,' I said. 'You're sure it was Mrs Hammond?'

'Yes. She had on a green dress, and I noticed her hair. I went back tonight to see if the lipstick was on the pavement. I couldn't find it. The street was crowded. Someone may have picked it up. It's three days ago. But I'm sure she had it when she fell.'

That was what I had not told Fred, that Elinor's gold lipstick was missing from her bag.

I looked at my watch. It was only eleven o'clock.

'We could go and look again,' I said.

She would not tell me her name. 'Just call me Smith. I don't want to get involved. I have a job to keep.'

I found the lipstick. It was at the side of the road, and twenty cars must have run over it. But after I wiped the mud off it, the familiar letter 'E' was there to see.

Miss Smith saw it and gasped. 'So I was right.'

Then she jumped on a bus, and I never saw her again.

I slept badly that night, and it was late when I got to Doctor Barclay's office the next morning. I walked in and put Elinor's lipstick on his desk.

'I don't think I understand,' he said, staring at it.

'Mrs Hammond was at the window using that lipstick, only a minute before she fell.'

'Do you mean it fell with her?'

'I mean that she never killed herself. Do you think a woman would put lipstick on just before she was going to do – what we're supposed to think she did?'

He smiled. 'My dear girl, if you saw as much of human nature as I do that wouldn't surprise you.'

'So Elinor Hammond jumped out of your window with a lipstick in her hand, and you watched the Hammond house last night and hurried away when I appeared. If that makes sense . . .'

It shocked him. He hadn't recognized me before.

'I see,' he said. 'So it was you.' He leaned forward in his chair. 'I suppose I'd better tell you and trust you to say nothing. I didn't like the way Mr Hammond looked at the inquest. I was afraid he might – well, shoot himself.'

'You couldn't stop it, standing outside,' I said.

'I was wondering how to get in when you arrived. His sister phoned me. She was worried.'

'I wouldn't rely too much on what Margaret Hammond says. She hated Elinor.' I stood up and picked up the lipstick.

'You're a very young and attractive woman, Miss Baring,' he said. 'Why don't you leave this alone? You can't bring her back, you know that.'

'I know she didn't kill herself,' I said.

I went out – and was less surprised than I might have been to find Margaret in the waiting room. She was standing close to the open window, and for one awful minute I thought she was going to jump herself.

'Margaret!' I said sharply.

She turned, and her face was white. 'Oh, it's you, Louise,' She sat down and wiped her face with her handkerchief. 'She must have slipped on the floor, Lou. It would be easy. Try it yourself.'

But I shook my head. I did not intend to look out of that open window with Margaret behind me. She said she had come to pay Fred's bill for Elinor, but there was something strange about her that day.

I had trouble starting my car, which is how I saw her leave the building. Then she did something that made me stop and watch her. She looked closely at the pavement and the side of the road. So she knew Elinor's lipstick had fallen with her. Or knew it was not in the bag.

She stopped a taxi and got into it. I don't know why I followed her, except she was the only suspect I had. The taxi went on and on, and I began to feel rather silly. Then it stopped and she got out. She went up some steps to a house and rang the bell.

She was in the house for almost an hour. But when she came out I sat up and stared. The woman at the door with her was

Mrs Thompson, from the inquest.

The taxi passed me but Margaret didn't even see my car. Mrs Thompson didn't go into the house at once and was still outside when I went up the steps.

'May I talk to you?' I said.

She was suspicious. 'What about?'

'A murder,' I said. 'I think you know something you didn't tell at the Hammond inquest.'

Some of the color went out of her face. 'It wasn't a murder,' she said. 'The verdict—'

'I think it was murder. What was Mr Hammond's sister doing here if it wasn't?'

'I never saw her before,' she said. 'She came to thank me for what I said at the inquest. Because it showed that the poor woman did it herself.'

'And to pay you for it, I suppose.'

'Nobody paid me anything,' she said angrily. 'If you think anybody can bribe me to lie, you're wrong!'

She went in and banged the door shut. Was she telling the truth? Was there something she had not said at the inquest? I was sure the doctor knew more than he had told. But why hide anything?

All afternoon I wondered what Doctor Barclay and the Thompson woman either knew or suspected. I also went to get my hair done at Elinor's hairdresser's. The girls there were very willing to talk about her, and I learned something new.

'I was waiting for her,' one of them said. 'Of course she never came, and—'

'You mean you expected her here the day it happened?'

'She had an appointment for four o'clock. When I heard what

58

happened, I couldn't believe it, although the last few weeks she hadn't been quite the same.'

'When did you notice a change in her?' I asked.

'About Easter. I remember I liked her new hat, and she gave it to me then and there! She said a strange thing. She said sometimes new hats were dangerous!'

My hair may have looked better when I left the hairdresser's, but my mind was going round in circles.

Mother and I invited Fred over for dinner that evening. During the meal I asked him if anything had happened to upset Elinor in the spring. 'About Easter,' I said.

'I don't remember anything,' he said. 'Except that she started going to that psychiatrist about then.'

'Why did she go to him, Fred?' mother asked.

'You saw him,' he said. 'He was good-looking. Maybe she liked to look at him instead of me.'

He went home soon after that.

I slept badly and was late for breakfast. Mother had finished reading the newspaper, and I took it.

The report was just a few lines on the back page. It said that Mrs Thompson had been shot the night before!

I couldn't believe it.

I read it again. She was not dead, but her condition was serious. She had been sitting alone outside her house when it happened. Nobody had heard the shot. Her husband found her when he came home at eleven o'clock. She had been shot through the chest and was still not able to make a statement.

'So she knew something that made her dangerous,' I thought. I remembered Margaret going up the steps to the house. Margaret searching for Elinor's lipstick in the street. Margaret, who hated Elinor. And I suddenly remembered Fred's gun, which he kept in his desk drawer.

I think it was the gun which finally made me go to the police. The police captain of the station wasn't interested, but a detective came to see me later.

'You don't think Mrs Hammond killed herself?' he said.

I told him about the lipstick, about Elinor's appointment at the hairdresser's, and that I thought Mrs Thompson knew something she hadn't told.

'Then who did it?' he said.

'I think it was Mr Hammond's sister. She was in Doctor Barclay's office yesterday, and insisted that Elinor had fallen out of the window. She said the floor was slippery, and she wanted me to try it myself.' I lit a cigarette and found that my hands were shaking. 'She also knew about the lipstick because I saw her trying to find it in the street.' But it was my next statement that made him really sit up. 'I think she was in the office the day Elinor was killed,' I said. 'I think the Thompson woman knew it. And I also think she went out there last night and shot her.'

He looked at me closely.

'Why do you think Miss Hammond shot her?' he said.

'Because she went to talk to her yesterday morning. She was there an hour. I know. I followed her.'

He stood up, his face expressionless. 'I have some advice for you, Miss Baring,' he said. 'Leave this to us. If you're right, then it's our job. If you're wrong, then no harm has been done. Not yet anyhow.'

I waited by the telephone that afternoon. When he called, it was to tell me that Mrs Thompson had now made a statement.

She did not know who shot her, or why, but insisted that Margaret had visited her only to thank her for being a witness at the inquest. She had not been given or offered any money.

But there was more. It seemed that Mrs Thompson had been worried since the inquest and had telephoned Margaret to ask her if it was important. Someone *had* entered the doctor's office while she was in the hall.

'The one person nobody really notices,' said the detective. 'The postman. I've talked to him. He saw Mrs Hammond in the office that morning. He remembers her. She had her hat off and was reading a magazine.'

'Did he see Mrs Thompson?'

'He didn't notice her, but she saw him.'

'So he went out last night and shot her!'

He laughed. 'He took his family to the movies last night. Remember, Miss Baring, that shot may have been an accident. Plenty of people are carrying guns now who never did before.'

So Elinor threw herself out of the window and Mrs Thompson was shot by somebody practicing their shooting! I didn't believe it. And I believed it even less after a visit from Doctor Barclay that night.

I had eaten dinner and was listening to the radio when he came. I told him about the police, and that surprised him.

'You've been to the police?' he said.

'Why not? Just because you don't want it known that somebody was pushed out of your office window—'

He was angry. 'You're dealing with something you don't understand. Why can't you stay out of this?'

I suppose I lost control then. 'How do I know you didn't do it?' I shouted. 'You or the postman!'

'The *postman*?' he said, staring. 'What do you mean?'

It must have been his surprised face which made me laugh. I laughed and laughed. Then I was crying, too. I couldn't stop. Suddenly, without warning, he hit me across the face. And that stopped me.

'Get out!' I told him, but he didn't move.

'Get out!' I told him, but he didn't move.

He had stopped looking angry; in fact he seemed rather pleased with himself. 'That's better,' he said, and patted me on the shoulder. 'I didn't come here to attack you. I came to ask you not to go out alone at night.'

'Why shouldn't I go out at night?'

'It may be dangerous,' he said, and I could see he was liking me less and less. 'I particularly want you to keep away from the Hammond house. And I hope you are sensible enough to do that.'

He banged the front door when he went out, and I was still angry when the telephone rang.

It was Margaret!

'I suppose we have you to thank for the police coming here tonight,' she said. 'We're in enough trouble without you making it worse!'

'All right,' I said dangerously. 'Now I'll ask you a question. Why did you visit Mrs Thompson yesterday morning? And who shot her last night?'

She gave a short gasp, then she put down the phone.

Mother had gone to bed and it was half an hour later when I found Fred standing at the kitchen door, smiling a tired smile. 'May I come in?' he said. 'I was out walking and I saw the light.'

He looked better, I thought. He said Margaret was in bed and the house was lonely.

'I don't sleep much anyway,' he said. 'And the house is hot. I've been getting rid of a lot of stuff. Burning it in the boiler.'

He smoked a cigarette and drank a cup of coffee, then I went out with him to the gates when he left, and watched as he started to walk home. I turned back towards the house and had almost reached it when it happened. I heard something move in the bushes and stopped to see what it was. But I never heard the shot. Something hit me on the head. I fell. Then everything went black.

The next thing I heard was my mother's voice. I was in my own bed with a bandage round my head.

'I think she's crazy,' mother was saying, very upset. 'She went out after you told her not to! Why can't she leave things alone?'

'I did my best, Mrs Baring,' said a male voice.

It was Doctor Barclay. He was standing by the bed. He looked strange. One of his eyes was almost shut, and his shirt collar was in a terrible state.

'You've been in a fight,' I said.

'Yes,' he said. 'And you've got a very pretty bullet graze on the side of your head. I've had to cut off quite a bit of your hair. Don't worry, it was very pretty hair and it will grow again.'

'Who did it? Who shot at me?'

'The postman,' he said, and went out of the room.

I slept after that. I suppose he gave me something. It was the next morning before I heard the rest of the story. He came in, big and smiling, with his right eye purple and completely closed. Then he told me.

In the spring, Elinor had come to him with a strange story. She was being followed, and was frightened. The man who was watching her, she said, wore a postman's uniform. It sounded fantastic, but she swore it was true.

'Do you mean it was this man that the Thompson woman saw going into your office?' I said.

'She's already identified him. The *real* postman had been there earlier. He had seen Mrs Hammond sitting in a chair, reading a magazine. But the real postman had gone before the Thompson woman arrived. The postman *she* saw was the one who, well, the one who killed Elinor.'

I knew before he told me. 'It was Fred, wasn't it?'

'It was Fred Hammond, yes.' He held my hand. 'I'm sorry, my dear. I tried to get Elinor to go away, but she wouldn't do it.'

'It's crazy. Fred was madly in love with her.'

'He loved her, yes. But he was afraid he was losing her. And he was wildly jealous.' He looked slightly embarrassed. 'I think he was jealous of me.'

'But if he really loved her—'

'The line between love and hate is a thin one. And it's possible he felt that she was never really his until – well, until no one else could have her.' He hesitated before going on. 'I was too late last night. I caught him just in time when he shot at you, but he put up a real battle. He got away somehow . . . and shot himself.'

He went on quietly. Mrs Thompson had identified Fred's photograph as the postman she had seen going into the office, and coming out again just before she heard the nurse screaming. The bullet she had been shot with had come from Fred's gun. And Margaret – poor Margaret – had been afraid that Fred had not been sane for some time.

'She came to see me yesterday after she heard the Thompson woman had been shot,' he said. 'She wanted Fred put away into a special hospital, but she almost went crazy when I talked about the police. I suppose there wasn't much proof, anyway. Mrs Thompson seemed to be dying and the uniform was gone—'

'Gone?' I said.

'He burned it in the boiler. We found some burned buttons and things last night.'

I tried to think. 'Why did he try to kill Mrs Thompson?' I said. 'What did she know?'

'She was able to describe the postman who went into my office. After Margaret heard this, she went home and searched the house. She found the uniform, and she knew. She tried to think what to do. But she had told Fred she was going to see Mrs Thompson that day and she thinks he knew she had found the uniform. All we know is that he left this house that night, got out his car, and tried to kill the only witness against him. Except you, of course.'

'But why should he try to kill me?' I said.

'Because you wouldn't leave things alone. You were a danger from the minute you insisted Elinor had been murdered. And because you telephoned Margaret last night and asked her why she had visited Mrs Thompson.'

'You think he was listening?'

'I know he was listening. And that was when Margaret sent me to warn you.' He admitted that he had been watching the Hammond house all evening, and that when Fred came to our kitchen door he had been just outside. But Fred had seemed quiet, drinking his coffee. Then Fred had begun to walk home, and he followed him behind the fence. But just too late he lost him, and he knew he was on the way back. Fred had lifted his gun to shoot me when he grabbed him.

Suddenly I found I was crying. It was all horrible. He got out a handkerchief and dried my eyes.

'It's all over now,' he said. 'You're a very brave woman, Louise Baring. Don't spoil it now.' He got up rather quickly. 'I think you've had enough of murder and sudden death. What you need is quiet. Someone will come soon to put a new bandage on your head.'

'Why can't you do it?'

'Because I'm not that sort of doctor.'

I looked up at him. He was tired and he needed a shave, and that awful eye was getting blacker. But he was big and strong and sane. A woman would be safe with him, I thought. Any woman. Although of course she could never tell him her dreams.

'Why can't you look after me?' I said. 'If I'm to look bald, I'd prefer you to see it. You did it.'

He smiled. Then to my surprise he kissed me lightly on the cheek. 'I've wanted to do that ever since you banged that lipstick down in front of me,' he said, 'And now will you stop being a detective and concentrate on growing some hair on the side of your head? Because I'm going to be around for a considerable time.'

When I looked up, mother was by the door, smiling.

Lazy Susan
NANCY PICKARD

'I want you to teach me how to shoot a gun,' Susan Carpenter said to her husband at breakfast.

'You want me to do *what*?'

Stan Carpenter stopped eating and stared at her.

'Take me to a shooting range.' Susan piled two tomatoes and a fried egg on to her bread so that she could eat it like a sandwich. It seemed to her a silly waste of effort to eat only one thing at a time.

Her husband's amazement turned to delight. 'I think that's a wonderful idea.' Ever since she'd been robbed the week before on a dark night in the parking-lot of the Mulberry Street Shopping Center, Stan had been telling her to learn how to protect herself, preferably with a gun. 'But do you mean it? You've always hated guns.'

'Well, I guess you win, dear,' said Susan, smiling.

'We'll go to the range tonight,' Stan promised.

Susan had been more angry than scared when she was robbed. The robber hadn't hurt her much, just a little knock on the head with his gun. It hadn't even broken the skin. But she was so angry about it!

'Fifty dollars!' she shouted at the nice policeman. 'One minute I had fifty dollars in my purse and then I had nothing! I have to work *hours* to earn that much money, and he takes it just like that! Fifty hard-earned dollars!'

She was right, of course, except about the 'hard-earned' part. Oh, she went to the sales office where she worked each day, and she smiled at the customers, and her bosses liked her – *most* people liked her, they couldn't help it. But there was more of her work that *didn't* get done than did. 'Oh, well,' she was always saying, 'you know me . . . Lazy Susan.'

'How does it feel?' said Stan.

'It feels OK,' said Susan. Actually, the little gun was surprisingly pleasant to hold. She lifted it and aimed it as Stan had instructed her, felt angry all over again at the thought of the robbery, and pulled the trigger.

'That's very good!' Stan shouted.

She'd never heard him shout before, but it was the only way of communicating at the Target Shooting Range. She wanted to point the gun at her mouth and blow the smoke away like John Wayne, but she didn't.

'Good evening, ladies.' The expert in self-defense stood beside a screen, and began by saying, 'The victim of a mugging usually looks like this . . .' A colored picture appeared on the screen. It was of a little old lady who was carrying a shopping bag in one hand and a purse in the other. 'She'll make it easy for the mugger to grab, push and run. He won't usually choose a victim who looks as if she might fight back.'

Another picture appeared on the screen – a younger woman, who looked strong, and whose hands were empty.

'If you want to avoid being mugged, walk confidently! Keep your head up. Pull your shoulders back. Let your arms swing, and don't carry a lot of packages. Carry your handbag under your arm, or hold it tightly with both hands. Look as if you know where you're going, even if you don't. Make that mugger think you're tough! Any questions?'

'Is there any way to recognize a mugger?' asked Susan.

'Sure.' The instructor smiled. 'He's the one in the dark clothes, hiding in the bushes.'

Everyone but Susan laughed.

This was the third evening she had come. The first evening they had learned to scream loudly and to run fast. The second evening they had learned how keys and nail scissors could be used as weapons. Now they had learned 'Who Is A Likely Mugging Victim?'

All the ladies who went home later held their heads high and didn't walk near any bushes.

Stan was amazed at how strong and confident Susan seemed after only three weeks of self-defense training. 'I've never seen you work so hard at anything,' he said.

'Well, some things are worth working hard at,' she said. 'And I'm still angry about being robbed!'

The shops were closed when the last movie-goers came out into the large, dark, Mulberry Street Shopping Center parking-lot. It had been a Superman film. After two and a half hours of watching him bend iron and jump over tall buildings, Susan felt ready for anything.

Stan would not have approved of her going to the movies alone, of course, especially not back to the 'scene of the crime'. But he was away, and now she knew a thing or two about looking after herself.

71

A dark group of bushes stood between her and her car. She walked confidently through them, then turned and bent down a little to look carefully behind her.

She saw the man before he noticed her.

Everything she had learned about self-defense went through her mind: she examined his walk, the look on his shadowed face, and the object in his hands. She thought of those hours she'd had to work to earn fifty dollars, and of the man who had stolen it from her so easily. She took from her pocket the little gun that Stan had taught her to use. Then, just as the man stepped past the bushes, she jumped behind him so he couldn't see her.

She put the gun against his head.

'I don't want to hurt you,' Susan said in her confident new voice, which sounded lower than normal. 'I just want your money.'

The little old man dropped his shopping bag beside one leg of Susan's trousers.

'There's been another mugging at the shopping center!' Stan folded back the local newspaper. The edges touched his fried egg. 'That just proves what I've said. You should never go there alone at night. You won't, will you, Susan?'

'You're getting egg on your trousers, dear.'

'What? Oh! It's all over the floor, too.'

'Don't worry about it,' said Susan. 'I'll clean it up. I have lots of extra time now.'

Stan smiled a little nervously. He was glad she had stopped doing that low-paying job at the sales office, but he was afraid his lovely but lazy Susan might not try very hard to find another job. 'You'll have time to train for something better,' he said,

'Yes, dear.' She smiled. 'I probably can.'

hopefully. 'I'm sure you can find an easier way to make money.'

Lazily, Susan stirred her coffee.

'Yes, dear.' She smiled. 'I probably can.'

The Gutting of Couffignal
DASHIEL HAMMETT

Couffignal is a two-hour ride from San Francisco. It is not a large island, and is joined to the mainland by a wooden bridge. Its western shore is a high, straight cliff that comes up out of Pablo Bay. From the top of the cliff the island slopes eastward to a beach, where there are piers and pleasure boats.

Couffignal's main street has the usual bank, hotel, movie theater and stores, but there are also trees and lawns, and no ugly flashing signs. The buildings seem to belong beside one another, as if they had been designed by the same person.

The streets that cross the main street run between rows of neat cottages near the bottom of the slope, but higher up the houses are larger and further apart. Most of the owners of these houses are rich, well-fed old men who will spend what is left of their lives nursing their health among their own kind. They admit to the island only as many storekeepers and working people as are needed to keep them comfortably served.

That is Couffignal.

It was some time after midnight. I was in an upstairs room in Couffignal's largest house, surrounded by wedding presents whose value would add up to something between fifty and a hundred thousand dollars. The ceremony had been performed in a little stone church down the hill. Then the house had begun to fill up with wedding guests, and had stayed filled until the bride and her new husband had gone off to catch their train.

74

A private detective at a wedding is supposed to look like any other guest, but this is never possible. He has to spend most of his time where he can see the presents, and what he is doing soon becomes obvious. Anyway, I recognized eight or ten of the guests as clients or former clients of mine.

Soon after dark a wind smelling of rain began to pile storm clouds up over the bay. Those guests who lived some distance away, especially those who had water to cross, hurried off for their homes. Those who lived on the island stayed until the first drops of rain began to fall. Then they left.

The Hendrixson house became quiet. Tired house servants disappeared to their bedrooms. I found some sandwiches, a couple of books and a comfortable chair, and took them up to the room where the presents were now hidden under a gray-white sheet.

Keith Hendrixson, the bride's grandfather (her parents were dead), put his head in at the door. 'Have you everything you need for your comfort?' he asked.

'Yes, thanks.'

He said good night and went off to bed – an old man, but tall and thin like a boy.

The wind was blowing and it was raining hard now. I pulled my chair close to a lamp, and put sandwiches, books, ashtray, gun and flashlight on a small table beside it. I lit a cigarette, made myself comfortable in the chair and picked up a book.

It was about a tough, violent man called Hogarth, whose modest plan was to hold the world in one hand. There were robberies and murders, escapes from prisons, and diamonds as large as hats. It sounds crazy, but in the book it was as real as a dollar.

Hogarth was still winning when the lights went out.

I pushed my cigarette into one of the sandwiches, put the book down, picked up the gun and flashlight, and moved away from the chair. Listening for noises was no good. The storm was making hundreds of them. I needed to know why the lights had gone off. All the other lights in the house had been turned off some time ago, so the darkness of the hall told me nothing.

I waited. My job was to watch the presents. Nobody had touched them yet.

Minutes went by, perhaps ten of them.

The floor moved under my feet. The windows shook violently. Then the sound of a heavy explosion filled the air, drowning out the noises of wind and falling water. It was not near, but nor was it off the island.

I walked over to the window. I should have been able to see a few misty lights far down the hill. *Not* being able to see them meant that the lights had gone out all over Couffignal, and not only in the Hendrixson house.

That was better. Maybe the storm had put out the lights, caused the explosion. Maybe.

I had an impression of great excitement down the hill, of movement in the night. But it was all too far away for me to have seen or heard anything even if there had been lights. I turned away from the window.

Another explosion spun me back to it. It sounded nearer than the first, maybe because it was stronger. Looking through the glass again, I still saw nothing.

The sound of bare feet hurrying came from the hall. A voice was anxiously calling my name. I put my gun in my pocket and switched on the flashlight. Keith Hendrixson, in night clothes and looking thinner and older than anybody could be, came into the room.

'Is it . . .?'

'I don't think it's an earthquake,' I said. That's the first disaster every Californian thinks of. 'The lights went off a little while ago. There have been a couple of explosions down the hill since—'

I stopped as I heard three shots, close together. Shots that only the heaviest of rifles could make. Then, sharp and small in the storm, came the sound of a handgun firing.

More feet were running in the hall. Excited voices whispered. A servant, partly dressed and carrying lighted candles, came in. He put the candles on the table beside my sandwiches.

'Brophy, will you try to find out what is the matter?' Hendrixson said to him.

'I have tried, sir. The telephone is not working. Shall I send Oliver down to the village?'

'No, I don't suppose it's that serious. Do you think it's anything serious?' Hendrixson asked me.

I said I didn't think so, but I had heard a thin scream that could have come from a distant woman, and the quick-firing of more shots. Then came the sound of the heavier guns again.

The doorbell rang suddenly – loud and long.

Brophy went away and came back.

'Princess Zhukovski,' he announced.

She ran into the room – a tall Russian girl who I had seen earlier at the wedding reception. Her eyes were wide and dark with excitement. Her face was very white and wet.

'Oh, Mr Hendrixson!' She was like an excited child. 'The bank is being robbed, and the chief of police is dead! When the explosion woke us, the general sent Ignati down to find out what was the matter. He got there in time to see the bank blown up. Listen!'

We heard a wild burst of mixed gunfire.

'That will be the general arriving at the bank!' she said. 'He'll enjoy himself wonderfully! As soon as Ignati returned with the news, the general gave a gun to every man in the house and led them out.'

'And the duchess?' Hendrixson asked.

'He left her at home with me, of course. I crept out of the house while she was trying to make tea. This is not the night to stay at home!'

Hendrixson looked at me. I said nothing.

'Could you do anything down there?' he asked.

'Maybe, but . . .' I nodded at the presents.

'Oh, those!' the old man said. 'I'm as interested in the bank as in them. And we'll be here.'

'OK, I'll go down. Leave Brophy in here, and put the chauffeur by the front door. Give them guns if you have any. Is there a raincoat I can borrow?'

Brophy found me a yellow rubber raincoat, then Hendrixson and the princess followed me downstairs. She was going with me.

'But Sonya!' the old man protested.

'I'm not going to be silly, though I'd like to,' she promised him. 'I'm going back to the duchess, who will perhaps have made some tea by now.'

'That's sensible,' Hendrixson said, and he let us out into the rain and the wind.

It wasn't the weather to talk in. We went down the hill, the storm driving at our backs. At the first break in the trees I stopped, nodding towards the black shape of a house. 'That is your—'

Her laugh stopped me. She took my arm and began to hurry me down the road again. 'I only told Mr Hendrixson that so he would not worry,' she explained.

She was tall. I am short and thick. I had to look up to see as much of her face as the rain-gray night would let me see. 'I don't know what we'll find down there,' I said. 'I can't look after you.'

'I can look after myself,' she said. 'I'm as strong as you, and quicker, and I can shoot.'

We hurried on.

Occasionally dark figures moved on the road ahead of us, but too far away to recognize anyone. Then a man passed us, running uphill.

'They've finished the bank and are at Medcraft's!' he shouted as he went by.

'Medcraft is the jeweler,' the girl informed me.

The houses were closer together now. Below, the occasional orange flash of a gun could be seen through the rain. We got to the main street just as a short, sharp RAT-TAT-TAT of gunfire broke out.

I pushed the princess into the nearest doorway, and jumped in after her. Bullets tore through walls, and I knew then that the RAT-TAT-TAT came from a machine gun.

The princess had fallen back in a corner, against a boy of about seventeen who was taking shelter in the doorway. He had one leg and a crutch.

'It's the boy who delivers newspapers,' Princess Zhukovski said, 'and you've hurt him.'

'What's happening?' I asked the paperboy.

The boy smiled as he got up. 'I'm not hurt, but you scared me, jumping on me like that.'

'What's happening?' I asked him.

'There must be a hundred of them,' he said. 'They've blown the bank wide open, and now some of them are in Medcraft's, and I guess they'll blow that up, too. And they killed Tom

Weegan. They've got a machine gun on a car in the middle of the street.'

'Where is everybody?'

'Most of them are up behind the Hall. The machine gun won't let them get near enough to see what they're shooting at. Bill Vincent told me to get out, because I've only got one leg – but I could shoot as good as anybody, if only I had something to shoot with.'

'You can do something for me,' I said. 'You can stay here and watch this end of the street, so I'll know if they leave in this direction.'

'You're not saying that to make me stay here out of the way, are you?' he said.

'No,' I lied. 'I need somebody to watch. I was going to leave the princess here, but you'll be better.'

'Yes,' she said, catching my idea. 'This man's a detective. Do what he asks, and you'll be helping more than if you were up with the others.'

The machine gun was still firing, but not in our direction now.

'I'm going across the street,' I told the girl.

'Aren't you going to join the others?'

'No. If I can get around behind the bandits, maybe I can do something useful.'

The princess and I ran across the street without getting shot at, then moved along the side of a building before turning into an alley. From the alley's other end came the smell of the bay.

The big figure of a man appeared ahead of us.

I stepped in front of the girl and went on towards him. Under my raincoat, I pointed my gun at his stomach. He stood still. He was larger than he had looked at first. His hands were empty. I

81

flashed the torch on his face for a second.

'Ignati!' the girl exclaimed over my shoulder.

He began to speak in Russian to her. She laughed at first, then shook her head and spoke sharply. He shook his head, then spoke to me.

'General Pleshskev, he tell me to bring Princess Sonya home.'

'Take her,' I said.

The girl looked angrily at me, then laughed. 'All right, Ignati,' she said in English, 'I shall go home.' And she turned and went back up the alley, the big man close behind her.

I moved on down to the beach, then went quickly along the shore towards the sounds of the machine gun and smaller gunfire. I heard three explosions, close together – bombs, hand grenades, I thought, remembering the sounds. That would be the jeweler's shop blowing apart. Another grenade went off. A man's voice screamed in terror.

I turned down to the water's edge. I had seen no dark shape on the water that could have been a boat. There had been boats along this beach in the afternoon. With my feet in the water of the bay I still saw no boat. The storm could have blown them away, but I didn't think it had. The wind was strong here, but not violent.

I went on up the shore. Now I saw a boat. A black shape ahead, with no lights. Nothing I could see moved on it. It was the only boat on that shore. That made it important.

A shadow moved between me and the dark back of a building. I stopped. The shadow, the size of a man, moved again, in the direction from which I was coming.

Twenty feet from me the shadow suddenly stopped.

I was seen. My gun was pointing at the shadow.

'Come on,' I said softly. 'Let's see who you are.'

The shadow came nearer. I couldn't risk using the flashlight, but I could just see a handsome face with a dark stain on one side of it. He was one of the Russians who had been at the wedding.

'Oh, how do you do?' the face's owner said lightly. 'You were at the wedding this afternoon.'

'Yes.'

'Have you seen Princess Zhukovski? You know her?'

'She went home with Ignati ten minutes ago.'

'Excellent!' He wiped his stained face with a stained handkerchief, and turned to look at the boat. 'That's Hendrixson's boat,' he whispered. 'They've got it, and they've got rid of the others.'

'That means they're going to leave by water.'

'Yes,' he agreed. 'Unless . . . shall we try . . .? There can't be many of them on the boat. God knows there are enough of them on shore. We both have guns.'

Staying close to the walls of the buildings, we crept towards the boat. It was about forty-five feet long, rising and falling in the water beside a small pier. There was something across the stern of the boat, but I couldn't see what it was. Moments later, a dark head and shoulders showed over the puzzling thing in the stern.

The young Russian's eyes were better than mine.

'He's wearing a mask over his face,' he whispered.

The man with the mask stood still. We stood still.

'Could you hit him from here?' the young Russian asked.

'Maybe,' I said. 'But better to get as close as we can, and start shooting when he sees us.'

Discovery came with our first step forward. The man in the boat made a low sound. The young man at my side jumped forward. I recognized the thing in the boat's stern just in time to throw out a leg and trip him. He fell down on the sand. I dropped behind him.

The machine gun in the boat's stern poured metal over our heads.

'Roll out of it!' I shouted.

I gave an example by rolling towards the back of the building we had just left.

The man at the gun fired wildly across the beach.

Around the corner of the building, we sat up.

'You saved my life by tripping me,' the young man said coolly.

'Yes. I wonder if they moved the machine gun from the street, or if this is another—'

The answer to that came immediately. The machine gun in the street joined its RAT-TAT-TAT with the one in the boat.

'A pair of them!' I said. 'And how many bandits?'

'I don't think there are more than ten or twelve of them,' he said, 'although it's not easy to count in the dark. The few I've seen are wearing masks, like the man in the boat. We attacked them while they were robbing the bank, but they had a machine gun on a car and we couldn't compete with that.'

'Where are the islanders now?'

'Hiding, I expect, unless General Pleshskev has succeeded in getting them together again.'

'Suppose you stay here and watch the boat,' I suggested. 'I'll see what's happening further up, and if I can get a few good men together I'll try to get on the boat again, probably from the other side.'

'You'll probably find most of the islanders up behind the church,' he said.

I moved off towards the main street where I stopped to look around before crossing it. Everything was quiet. The only man I could see was lying face down on the ground near me. I crawled to his side on my hands and knees and looked at him. He was dead.

I jumped up and ran to the other side of the street. Nothing tried to stop me. In a doorway, flat against a wall, I looked out carefully. The wind had stopped, and the rain was now a steady downpour of small drops. Couffignal's main street was empty.

I walked quickly towards the bank. From high up on the hill I could hear a machine gun throwing out its stream of bullets. Mixed with this noise were the sounds of smaller guns, and a grenade or two.

I left the main street and began to run up the hill. Men were running towards me. Two of them passed, but I stopped the third one. He was white-faced and breathing hard.

'They've moved the car with the machine gun up behind us,' he gasped. 'Back there somewhere. He's trying to take the car, but he'll never do it.'

Other men had passed us, running downhill, as we talked. I let the white-faced man go, and stopped four men who weren't running as fast as the others.

'What's happening now?' I asked.

'They're going through the houses up the hill,' a sharp-faced man with a gun said.

'Has anybody taken the news off the island yet?'

'Can't,' another said. 'They blew up the bridge.'

'Can't anybody swim?'

'Not in that wind.'

'The wind's quieter now,' I said.

The sharp-faced man gave his gun to one of the others and took off his coat. 'I'll try it,' he said.

'Good! Wake up the whole country, and get the news through to the San Francisco police boat. Tell them the bandits have a boat with a machine gun ready to leave in. It's Hendrixson's.'

The sharp-faced man left.

'A boat?' two of the men asked together.

'Yes. If we're going to do anything, it'll have to be now. Get every man and every gun you can find down there. Shoot at the boat from the roofs if you can. When the bandit's car comes down, shoot into it. You'll do better from the buildings than from the street.'

A hundred yards further on, what was left of the general's men came out of the night, running downhill, with bullets flying after them. I got off the road into soft, wet grass, and continued my uphill journey. The machine gun on the hill was silent. The one in the boat was still at work.

The one ahead started again, firing too high to hit anything near. It was helping its partner below, shooting into the main street.

Before I could get closer it had stopped. I heard the car moving towards me. Rolling into the trees, I lay there. I had six bullets. When I saw wheels on the road, I emptied my gun, firing it low.

The car went on.

I jumped out of my hiding place.

The car was suddenly gone from the empty road.

There was a loud crash. The noise of metal folding on itself. The sound of breaking glass.

I ran towards those sounds.

Out of a black pile where an engine coughed and died, a black figure jumped – and ran off across the wet lawn. I went after it, hoping that the others in the wreck were dead.

I was about ten yards behind the running man. I was tempted to throw my empty gun at his head, but it was too risky. A dark building appeared. My man ran to the right, to get around the corner.

To the left, a heavy gun went off.

The running man disappeared around the house corner.

'Sweet God!' General Pleshskev's voice complained. 'How could I miss him at that distance?'

'Go round the other way!' I shouted, running around the corner after my man.

His feet ran on ahead. I could not see him. The general came around from the other side of the house.

'You have him?'

'No.'

In front of us was a stone-faced bank, on top of which was a path. On either side of us were high and solid bushes. A pale triangle showed on the path above – a triangle that could have been a bit of shirt above the opening of a jacket.

'Stay here and talk!' I whispered to the general, and crept forward.

'He must have gone the other way,' the general said, as if I were standing beside him, 'because if he had come this way I should have seen him, and if he had raised himself above the bushes, one of us would have seen him against . . .'

He talked on and on while I climbed the stone bank. The man on the path, trying to make himself small with his back in a bush, was looking at the general. He saw me when I had my feet on the path.

He jumped, and one hand went up.

I jumped, with both hands out.

A stone, turning under my foot, threw me sideways, saving my head from the bullet he sent at it.

As I went down, my arm caught his legs and he came down on top of me. I kicked him once, caught his gun arm, and had just decided to bite it when the general came across the path and pushed the man off me with his gun.

I stood up. I had hurt my ankle and it was difficult to stand. I put most of my weight on the other leg and turned my flashlight on the prisoner.

'Hello, Flippo!' I exclaimed.

'Hello,' he said, not happy to be recognized.

He was a fat Italian of twenty-three or four. I'd helped send him to prison four years ago for his part in a robbery. He had been out for several months now.

'The prison board isn't going to like this,' I told him.

'You've got it wrong,' he said. 'I wasn't doing anything. I was up here to see some friends. And when this thing broke loose I had to hide. If the police catch me here I'll be in trouble. And now you've got me and you think I'm part of it.'

'You're a mind reader,' I told him, and asked the general, 'Where can we lock him away for a while?'

'In my house there's a room with a strong door and no windows,' said the general.

He took Flippo's arm while I walked painfully behind him, re-loading my gun. We didn't have far to go. The general knocked on the door of his house and called out something in his language. The door was opened by a Russian servant with a heavy mustache. Behind him were the princess and an older woman.

We took Flippo up to the room with no windows as the general told the others what had happened. We locked our prisoner inside, then went downstairs.

'You are hurt!' the princess said to me.

'I turned my foot over, that's all. But it would be better with some support. Do you have a bandage?'

'Yes,' she said, and spoke to the servant, who went out of the room and returned with a bandage.

There was no sound of gunfire coming up the hill now, and the rain was lighter. The night was almost over, and it would soon be day. I had tied the bandage round my ankle and was fastening the button on my raincoat when there was a knock on the front door. I heard someone speaking in Russian, then the young Russian I had met on the beach came in.

'Aleksander, you're—!' the older woman screamed when she saw the blood on his face, and fainted.

He took no notice of this, as if he was used to her fainting. 'They've gone in the boat,' he told me, while the girl and two servants picked the woman up and laid her on a sofa.

'How many?' I asked.

'I counted ten.'

'The men I sent down there couldn't stop them?'

He lifted his shoulders and let them drop again. 'It takes a strong stomach to face a machine gun.'

The woman who had fainted was now asking questions in Russian. The princess was putting on her coat. The woman stopped questioning the young man and asked her something.

'It's all over,' the princess said. 'I'm going to look at the wreckage.'

That idea appealed to everybody. Five minutes later all of us were on our way downhill. Other islanders were hurrying down in the rain, too, their faces tired and excited in the morning light.

A woman ran out of the crowd and began to tell me something. I recognized her as one of Hendrixson's maids. I caught some of her words.

'Presents gone . . . Mr Brophy murdered . . . Oliver . . .'

'I'll be down later,' I told the others, and went after the maid.

She was running back to the Hendrixson house. I couldn't run, or walk fast. She and Hendrixson and more of his servants were outside when I arrived.

'They killed Oliver and Brophy,' the old man said.

'How?'

'We were in the back of the house, upstairs, watching the shooting down in the village. Oliver was just inside the front door, and Brophy in the room with the presents. We heard a shot in there, and immediately a man appeared in the doorway of our room, threatening us with two guns, making us stay there for perhaps ten minutes. Then he shut and locked the door and went away. We broke the door down – and found Brophy and Oliver dead.'

'Let's look at them.'

The chauffeur was just inside the front door. He lay on his back, with this throat cut straight across the front. His gun was under him. I pulled it out and examined it. It had not been fired.

Upstairs, Brophy was lying against a leg of one of the tables on which the presents had been spread. His gun was gone. There was a bullet hole in his chest.

Most of the presents were still there. But the most valuable ones were gone.

'What did the man you saw look like?' I asked.

'I didn't see him very well,' Hendrixson said. 'There was no light in our room. He was just a large man in a black rubber raincoat, and wearing a black mask.'

As we went downstairs again, I told Hendrixson what I had seen and heard and done since I had left him.

'Do you think you can get information about the others from the one you caught?' he asked, as I prepared to go out.

'No. But I expect to catch them.'

Couffignal's main street was full of people when I got down to it again. Some men from the San Francisco police boat were there. A hundred voices were all talking at once.

The bank had been completely wrecked, and so had the jeweler's shop. Two doctors were helping the injured villagers. I recognized a familiar face under a uniform hat – Sergeant Roche of the harbor police – and pushed through the crowd to him.

'What do you know?' he asked as we shook hands.

'Everything.'

'Who ever heard of a private detective who didn't?' he joked as I led him out of the crowd.

'Did your people see an empty boat out in the bay?' I asked when we were away from audiences.

'Empty boats have been floating around the bay all night,' he said.

I hadn't thought of that. 'Where's your boat now?'

'Out trying to catch the bandits. I stayed with a couple of men to help here.'

'You're in luck,' I told him. 'See the old man across the street with the black beard?'

General Pleshskev stood there, with the woman who had fainted, the young Russian whose bloody face had made her faint, and a pale, fat man of forty-something who had been with them at the wedding. Near them stood Ignati, two men-servants I had seen at the house, and another who was obviously one of them.

'Yes, I see your man with the beard,' said Roche.

'Well he's one of the people you want. And so are the woman and the two men with him. And those four Russians standing to the left are more of them. There's another missing, but I'll take care of that one. Pass the information to your chief, and you can catch them before they get a chance to fight back. They think they're safe.'

'Are you sure?'

'I'm sure.'

I began to move through the crowd to the other side of the street. The princess didn't seem to be among those present. My idea was that, next to the general, she was the most important member of the gang. If she was at the house, and she did not suspect anything, I guessed she would not give me too much of a fight.

Walking was hell. The pain from my ankle went straight up my leg, like a knife.

'None of them came down that way,' a voice said.

The newspaper boy with one leg was standing by my elbow. I greeted him as if he was my pay check.

'Come with me,' I said, taking his arm. 'You did well down there, and now I want you to do something else for me.'

I led him to the doorway of a small yellow cottage. The door was open, left that way when the owners ran down to welcome the police, I guessed. Just inside the door was a chair. I pulled the chair outside.

'Sit down, son,' I told the boy. Then I took his crutch out of his hand. 'Here's five dollars to rent it, and if I lose it I'll buy you one made of gold.'

I put the crutch under my arm and began to push myself up the hill. The hill was longer and steeper than some mountains I've seen, but the path to the Russians' house was finally under my feet.

I was still about twelve feet from the house when Princess Zhukovski opened the door.

'Oh!' she exclaimed. And then, recovering from her surprise, said, 'Your ankle is worse!' She ran down the steps to help me climb them, and I noticed she had something heavy in the right-hand pocket of her jacket. With one hand under my elbow, she helped me into the house. Why, I wondered, had she come back to the house after starting to go down with the others?

She put me in a soft leather chair. 'You must be hungry,' she said. 'I will see—'

'No, sit down.' I nodded at a chair opposite mine. 'I want to talk to you.'

She sat down. She did not look nervous, or even curious. And that was her big mistake.

'Where have you hidden it all?' I asked.

Her face was white, but it had been like that since I first saw her. Her voice was smoothly cool.

'I don't understand your question,' she said.

'I'm charging you with helping in the gutting of Couffignal, and with the murders,' I explained. 'I'm asking you where the things you stole are hidden.'

Slowly, she stood up and looked at me. 'How dare you speak to me like that! Me, a Zhukovski!'

'I don't care who you are,' I told her. 'You're a thief and a murderer.'

Her white face became the face of a wild animal. One hand – claw now – went to the heavy pocket of her jacket. Then, as quick as a flash, the animal had disappeared. And there was the princess again, cool and in control.

She sat down, crossed her ankles, put an elbow on an arm of her chair, put her chin on the back of that hand, and looked curiously into my face.

'How did you get an idea as strange and fantastic as that?' she murmured.

'It's not strange or fantastic,' I said. 'First – whoever planned the job knew the island, every inch of it. Second – the car on which the machine gun was fixed was local property, stolen from the owner here. So was the boat in which the bandits were supposed to have escaped. Bandits from outside the island would have needed a car or a boat to bring their machine guns and grenades here. So why didn't they use that car or boat instead of stealing a fresh one? Third – this job wasn't the work of professional bandits. The worst burglar in the world could have robbed the bank and the jeweler's without wrecking the buildings. Fourth – bandits from the outside wouldn't have destroyed the bridge. They might have blocked it, but they wouldn't have destroyed it. They might have wanted to make their getaway in that direction. Fifth – bandits planning on a getaway by boat would have cut the job short, not spread it over the whole night. Enough noise was made here to wake

California all the way from Sacramento to Los Angeles. What you people did was send one man out in the boat, shooting, and he didn't go far. As soon as he was at a safe distance, he swam back to the island. Big Ignati could have done it easily.'

I stopped counting with my right hand, and began counting on my left.

'Sixth – I met one of your men, the young man, down on the beach, and he was coming from the boat. He suggested that we tried to get on the boat, and we were shot at, but the man behind the gun was playing with us. He shot over our heads. He could have killed us in a second if he had wanted to. Seventh – that same young man is the only person on the island, as far as I know, who saw the departing bandits. Eighth – all of your people were very nice to me. The general even spent an hour talking to me at the wedding this afternoon. No professional criminal would do that. Ninth – after the machine gun car had been wrecked, I chased its occupant. I lost him around this house. The Italian boy I caught wasn't him. He couldn't have climbed up on the path without my seeing him. But he could have run around to the general's side of the house and disappeared indoors. The general was obviously helping him, because his shot managed to miss him from less than six feet away. Tenth – you only called at Hendrixson's house to get me away from there.'

That finished my left hand. I went back to my right.

'Eleventh – Hendrixson's two servants were killed by someone they knew and trusted. I'd guess you got Oliver to let you into the house, and were talking to him when one of your men cut his throat from behind. Then you went upstairs and shot the unsuspecting Brophy yourself. Twelfth – but that ought to be enough. I'm getting a sore throat from listing them.'

She took her chin off her hand, took a cigarette out of a thin black case, and held it in her mouth while I put a match to the end of it. She took a long pull at it and blew the smoke down at her knees.

'That *would* be enough,' she said, 'except that it would have been impossible for us to do all those things. You saw us – everyone saw us – many times.'

'That's easy!' I argued. 'With a couple of machine guns, grenades, knowing the island from top to bottom, in the darkness and in a storm – it was easy for you. There are nine of you that I know about, including two women. Any five of you could have done the work, once it was started, while the others appeared here and there providing alibis. Everywhere I went, there was one of you. And the general! That old joker running around leading the islanders to battle! They're lucky that there are any of them alive this morning!'

She finished her cigarette. 'And now what?'

'Now I want to know where you have hidden the things you stole.'

I was surprised by how ready she was to answer.

'Under the garage. We secretly dug a place there some months ago.'

I didn't believe that, of course, but I learned later it was true.

I didn't have anything else to say, so I picked up the crutch, preparing to stand up.

'Wait a moment, please,' she said. 'I have something to suggest.'

Half standing, I held out a hand. 'I want the gun.'

She nodded, and sat still while I took it from her pocket, put it in one of my own, and sat down again.

'You said a little while ago that you didn't care who I was,' she began. 'But I *want* you to know. There are so many of us Russians who were once important people but who are now

'How did you get an idea as strange as that?' she murmured.

nobodies. We were forced to leave Russia with what we could carry of our property. In London we opened a Russian restaurant, but London was suddenly full of Russian restaurants. We tried teaching music and languages, but found that too many other Russians were doing the same thing. Our money was almost gone. There was no place for us in the world. It was *easy* to become a criminal. Why not? Did we owe the world anything? The world had watched as we were robbed of our place and property and country.

'We planned it before we had heard of Couffignal. We would find a small group of wealthy people, suitably isolated, and after becoming accepted and trusted by everyone, we would rob them. Couffignal seemed to be the ideal place. We had just enough money to rent this house for six months. We spent four months getting ourselves accepted by the people here, collecting our guns and grenades, waiting for a suitable night. Last night seemed to be that night, and we thought we were prepared for anything that could happen. But we weren't prepared for you – a clever and observant detective – being here on the island.'

'The truth is that you made mistakes from beginning to end,' I said. 'You people have no criminal experience, but you tried to do a job that needed the highest criminal skills. Look at how you all played around with me! A professional criminal with any intelligence would have either left me alone or murdered me. And the rest of your troubles? I can't do anything about them.'

'Why can't you?' she said softly, putting a white hand on my knee. 'There is wealth beneath the garage. You can have whatever you ask.'

I shook my head.

'You aren't a fool!' she protested. 'You know—'

'Let me tell you something,' I interrupted. 'We won't talk about whatever honesty I have, or loyalty to my employers. You might doubt them, so we'll forget them. I'm a detective because I happen to like the work. I could find jobs that would pay more, but I like the work. And liking the work makes you want to do it as well as you can. Money is nice. I haven't anything against it. But in the past eighteen years I've got my fun out of chasing criminals and solving puzzles. It's the only kind of sport I know anything about, and I can't imagine a pleasanter future than twenty years more of it. I'm not going to wreck that!'

She shook her head slowly, looking at me with her dark eyes. 'You speak only of money,' she breathed. 'I said you can have whatever you ask.'

That was out. I don't know where these women get their ideas.

I stood up. 'You don't understand do you? You think I'm a man and you're a woman. That's wrong. I'm a hunter and you're something that's been running in front of me. We're wasting time. I've been thinking the police might come up here and save me a walk. You've been waiting for your friends to come back and get me. I could have told you they were being arrested when I left them.'

That surprised her. She stood up, fell back a step, and put a hand on her chair. She said something I didn't understand. Something Russian, I thought, but the next moment I knew it had been Italian.

'Put your hands up!' It was Flippo's voice. He stood in the doorway, holding a gun.

I raised my hands as high as I could without dropping my crutch. So this was why she had come back to the house! If she freed the Italian, we would have no reason for suspecting that he hadn't been one of the criminals, and so we would look for the bandits among his friends. But as a prisoner, he might have persuaded us he was innocent. She had given him the gun so that he could either shoot his way out, or get himself killed trying.

Flippo took my gun away, and the gun I had taken from the girl.

'A bargain, Flippo,' I said. 'You're in trouble with the police. You could easily be sent back to prison if I tell them I found you carrying a gun. But I know you weren't part of this job. I think you were up here on a smaller one of your own. But I can't prove that and I don't want to. Walk out of here alone and I'll forget I saw you.'

Flippo thought about this.

The princess moved nearer to him. 'You heard what I offered him?' she said. 'Well, I make this offer to you, if you will kill him.' Then she said something hot and heavy in Italian. He listened, breathing harder. 'Well?' she said. He was young and she was beautiful. His answer wasn't hard to guess.

'But not to kill him,' he said in English. 'We'll lock him in the room I was in.'

The girl wasn't satisfied with this suggestion. She spoke more hot Italian to him. She was depending on her charm to persuade him. And that meant she had to keep him looking at her.

He wasn't far from me.

She came near to him. She was whispering Italian words into his round face.

His whole face said yes. He turned—

I knocked him on the head with my borrowed crutch.

100

The crutch broke. Flippo's knees bent. He fell on his face on the floor, and a thin stream of blood crawled out of his hair on to the carpet.

A step, a fall, some hand-and-knee movements, put me within reach of Flippo's gun.

The girl, jumping out of my path, was halfway to the door when I sat up with the gun in my hand.

'Stop!' I ordered.

'I shan't,' she said, but she did, for the moment at least. 'I am going out.'

'You are going out when I take you.'

She laughed, a pleasant laugh, low and confident.

'I'm going out before that,' she said.

I shook my head.

'How will you stop me?' she asked.

'I don't think I'll have to. You're too sensible to try to run when I'm pointing a gun at you.'

She laughed again. 'I'm too sensible to stay. Your crutch is broken. You can't run after me. You pretend you'll shoot me, but I don't believe you.'

She looked over her shoulder, her dark eyes smiling at me, and moved towards the door.

'Stop, you fool!' I shouted at her.

She walked steadily to the door. I took a deep breath and my hand tightened on the gun. When her right foot was in the doorway, a little laughing sound came from her throat.

'Goodbye!' she said softly.

And I put a bullet in her left leg.

She sat down – bump! Complete surprise stretched her white face. It was too soon for pain.

I had never shot a woman before. It felt strange.

'You ought to have known I'd do it!' My voice sounded hard and angry, and like a stranger's in my ears. 'Didn't I steal a crutch from a cripple?'

GLOSSARY

alibi the proof that you were elsewhere when a crime happened

ashtray a small metal or glass bowl for the ash from cigarettes

bandit a robber

boiler a big metal container with a fire, used to provide hot water

chauffeur someone employed to look after and drive a person's car

clerk a person who works in a bank, office, or store

client someone who goes to a professional person for help

cop a policeman

coroner an official responsible for the investigation of violent or sudden deaths

cripple someone who cannot move their body properly because of an injury, illness, or disease

crutch a long stick placed under the arm to help a person who has difficulty in walking

duchess the wife or widow of a duke

executed put to death as a punishment

fiancé (fiancée) the man (woman) you are engaged to marry

fingerprint a mark made by a finger showing the lines on the skin

flashlight an electric torch

fool *(v)* to deceive

gasoline/gas petrol (fuel for cars)

governess a woman employed by a family to educate their children

graze *(n)* a scratch or slight injury to the skin

gutting robbing, often accompanied by burning and destroying

hairdresser a person who washes and cuts people's hair

hand grenade a small container filled with explosive and thrown by hand

hypocrite a person who pretends to believe or feel something they do not

inquest the official inquiry to find out the cause of someone's death

lawn an area of short, regularly cut grass in a garden or park

lipstick something which women put on their lips to color them

liquor store a shop that sells liquor (alcohol)

machine gun a gun which fires bullets quickly and automatically

maid a woman servant

mainland the main part of the land, not an island

make-up things like powder, lipstick, eye-shadow, etc. which women use on their faces

mourning showing great sadness and wearing dark clothes because of someone's death

movie (the movies) a film (a cinema)

mugging a street robbery

nursery a children's room

omelet a dish of cooked eggs

package a parcel

parking-lot a car park

pier a platform of wood or metal, built out into the sea

pill a small, round, hard piece of medicine which is swallowed

press to push hard against something

princess the daughter of a king or queen, or the wife of a prince

psychiatrist a doctor for illnesses of the mind

pump *(v)* to force liquid, air, etc. into or out of something

purse a woman's handbag

radiator something used to heat a room; part of a heating system

range *(n)* a place where people can practice shooting guns

reference a letter to an employer describing the character and
    capabilities of an applicant for a job
rifle a kind of long gun, usually held against the shoulder
ruffle to push a hand quickly and gently through someone's hair
    (often to show fondness for that person)
sane not mad
scared very frightened
stern *(n)* the back of a boat
suicide a person who deliberately kills himself or herself
tank a large metal container
tattoo a picture or design on someone's skin, made with a needle
trailer a caravan
trigger the part of a gun which you pull to fire it
wig a covering for the head made of false hair

Before Reading

1 **Read the introduction on the first page of the book, and the back cover. What can you guess about these stories?**

Death Wish
What will the man leaning over Morrissey Bridge do?
a) Kill himself   b) Kill somebody else   c) Pay for a murder

Death on Christmas Eve
Who does the murderer kill on Christmas Eve?
a) A stranger   b) A lover   c) A relation

The Heroine
What does 'the heroine' of the story want to save people from?
a) A fire   b) A gunfight   c) A kidnapping

Ride the Lightning
Who goes to the electric chair?
a) Curtis Colt   b) Curtis's girlfriend   c) Somebody else

The Lipstick
What does Louise find on the lipstick?
a) Fingerprints   b) Poison   c) The owner's initials

Lazy Susan
What is the result of Susan's laziness?
a) Murder   b) Armed robbery   c) Burglary

The Gutting of Couffignal
What is the motive behind the armed attack on Couffignal?
a) Hate   b) Revenge   c) Hunger

While Reading

Read *Death Wish*, and then answer these questions.

Why

1 ... didn't the cop run to stop the man from jumping off the bridge?
2 ... did the man tell the cop his name?
3 ... did the man tell the psychiatrist about his dream?
4 ... didn't Edward Wright's wife run away with Mark?
5 ... did Edward Wright kill his wife?
6 ... did Edward Wright write a suicide note?
7 ... was Mark sure that Wright's friends would say he was suicidal?

Read to the bottom of page 17 in *Death on Christmas Eve*. Can you guess the answer to this question?

Who will be alive in the Boerum House at the end of the story?
a) Only Celia   b) Only Charlie   c) Both of them   d) Nobody

Now read to the end of the story and answer these questions.

1 Why was Celia cleared of Jessie's murder at the inquest?
2 How was Celia like her mother?
3 Why did the lawyer stay behind Celia until he left the house?
4 Celia ran along as if she was 'being chased by something'. Who or what do you think that was?
5 Why was Al Sharp expecting the lawyer to come into his bar?
6 Why did the lawyer say, 'Jessie will always be with them'?

Read *The Heroine*. This summary is full of mistakes. Rewrite it with the correct information.

Before Lucille bought the Christiansens' house, she had worked as a teacher in different schools for ten years. Her father had died three weeks earlier, but he had not been sane for a year. Lucille too had been sent to prison for attacking people, but the Christiansens knew all about her past.

Lucille enjoyed her work and liked the animals, though she wanted to work less hard for more pay. But she felt she wanted to do something foolish to prove how little she cared about the family. So late one morning she used a bomb to blow up the house, hoping that this would give her the chance to save the animals and be a heroine.

Read *Ride the Lightning*. Who said this, and to whom? Who or what were they talking about?

1 'Curtis doesn't belong in it, and I can prove it.'
2 'Why should I worry about it any more?'
3 'The jury didn't believe it. Neither do I.'
4 'They don't want to live knowing they might have made a mistake and killed an innocent man.'
5 'Watching her trailer would be a waste of time.'
6 'He's somebody you paid to sit there and lie to me.'
7 'Yours will stay with you for years.'

Read to the bottom of page 61 in *The Lipstick*. Can you guess the answer to this question?

Who killed Elinor and shot Mrs Thompson?
a) Dr Barclay   b) Margaret   c) Fred   d) Someone else

Now read to the end of the story. Choose the best question-word for these questions and then answer them.

What / Who / Why

1 . . . kind of person was Elinor?
2 . . . did Louise suspect of killing Elinor, and why?
3 . . . did Doctor Barclay come to see Louise?
4 . . . three things did Fred do in an attempt to prevent discovery?
5 . . . happened in Louise's garden after Fred left?

Read *Lazy Susan*. Here are some untrue sentences about the story. Change them into true sentences.

1 Susan had felt frightened because the robber hurt her badly.
2 The typical mugging victim is a man in dark clothes.
3 After three weeks of self-defense training Susan still didn't feel like going out alone.
4 Susan planned to get another office job with better pay.

Read *The Gutting of Couffignal*. Are these sentences true (T) or false (F)? Rewrite the false ones with the correct information.

1 The first sign that something was wrong was a heavy explosion.
2 The robbers attacked the bank first, then the jeweler's.
3 One man took the news to the mainland by running across the bridge.
4 The robbers left the island on Hendrixson's boat.
5 The wedding presents were stolen but nobody was killed.
6 The detective realized that the robbers came from the island.
7 The Russians lacked the right criminal skills for the robbery.
8 The princess's friends had already escaped from the island when the detective shot her in the back.

After Reading

1 Perhaps this is what some of the characters in the stories were thinking. Which seven characters were they (one from each story), and what was happening in the story at that moment?

   1 'How easy that was – and how quick! It used to take me *ages* to get that much, and now it just takes minutes. Well, I know what I'm going to do first thing tomorrow. I'm going to give up my job. Work is for idiots!'

   2 'Perhaps we should have phoned the Howells, but it didn't really seem necessary. She's so young and keen. She does seem a bit nervous, but it's her first day, so that's natural. I'm sure the children are going to like her. I'll leave them to have lunch together now . . .'

   3 'That went very well. I was a bit worried about the signature, but he didn't seem to notice anything. I've got everything I need, and I've seen everyone I need to see, so now there's only one more thing for me to do. It's time to pay a little visit . . .'

   4 'She's so pretty – even when she's shouting at me or crying! I'm worried about her, though. She won't stop asking questions. I do hope she takes my advice and stays indoors. Now I'd better get back to the house and see what's happening there . . .'

   5 'This one's too smart for us, and he's not interested in money. But there must be *something* he wants. I've got to keep him busy until the others get back here. Well, he's a handsome man – perhaps he'd be interested in me . . .'

6 'I can hear him coming now. He's got to listen to me. He's got to tell me what to do! I can't bear it any longer. Surely everyone can see that she's guilty? So why can't they take her away from here, and do what has to be done? There must be a way . . .'

7 'The car. That's what's been bothering me. She went home from the funeral by taxi, and I've never seen a car outside the trailer. But she must have one – how does she get to work otherwise? So where is it? I think I'll get down there and start watching tomorrow morning . . .'

2 Here are Celia and Charlie, from *Death on Christmas Eve*, having one of their regular arguments. Complete Charlie's side of the conversation (use as many words as you like).

CELIA: Christmas always makes me sad, because it makes me think of poor dear Jessie. I loved her so much.

CHARLIE: _____

CELIA: No, Charlie, it's the truth. I did not hate her, and I was very sorry when she died.

CHARLIE: _____

CELIA: Her death was a terrible accident, Charlie. How many times do I have to tell you that?

CHARLIE: _____

CELIA: Jessie and I *never* argued, and we didn't argue that day. She just slipped and fell down the stairs.

CHARLIE: _____

CELIA: How could I have done it? I was in my room when she fell.

CHARLIE: _____

CELIA: Yes, she screamed because she was falling down the stairs. But that still doesn't mean I pushed her.

3 **At the end of** *The Heroine,* **what do you think happens next? Choose one of these ideas (or think of one of your own) and write a new ending for the story.**

As though this was the sign for which she had been waiting, Lucille went confidently forward . . .

- goes into house / dies with family in flames / 'terrible tragedy' / person responsible for fire unknown
- calls fire brigade / children die, parents rescued / police find evidence / Lucille guilty of murder
- runs into house / rescues children / parents die in fire / famous heroine / cured of illness

4 *The Lipstick* **could have been a very different story. What might have happened if . . .? Complete these sentences in your own words.**

1 If Elinor hadn't married Fred, . . .
2 If Louise hadn't noticed that the lipstick was missing, . . .
3 If the office girl hadn't seen Elinor putting on lipstick, . . .
4 If Mrs Thompson had died, . . .
5 If Louise hadn't telephoned Margaret about Mrs Thompson, . . .
6 If Margaret hadn't sent Dr Barclay to warn Louise, . . .
7 If Fred hadn't murdered his wife, . . .

5 **What was Holly Ann thinking, at the end of** *Ride the Lightning*? **Here are her thoughts after Nudger left. Choose one suitable word to fill each gap.**

Nudger's right. He can't _____ anything, but he's right _____ what happened. I was _____ one, God help me, _____ did the shooting. I _____ want to, but I _____ no choice. The old _____ went crazy

and ran _____ me, and when I'd _____ him, his wife went _____
too. Every time I _____ my eyes, I see _____ old woman's face as
_____ fell. It should have _____ me in that electric _____. Curtis
didn't deserve to _____, and I'm going to _____ to live, knowing he
_____ me, and I killed _____. It doesn't matter how _____ whisky I
drink, I _____ stop thinking about it . . .

6 **Here is the report that the detective in *The Gutting of Couffignal*
wrote for Sergeant Roche. Put the parts of sentences in the right
order, and join them with these linking words to make a paragraph
of five sentences.**

*and / and / as / because / before / however / where / while / while /
who*

1 _____ stole the most valuable wedding presents.
2 _____ they waited for a suitable night to rob the island.
3 The Russians rented a house in Couffignal six months ago
4 _____ I found and shot Princess Zhukovski,
5 On the night of the storm, some of them attacked the bank and
   the jeweler's,
6 _____ they killed two servants
7 _____ the police would look for criminals
8 Then the Russians began robbing the houses, including the
   Hendrixson house,
9 _____ she was trying to escape.
10 _____ began making friends and collecting weapons
11 The Russians thought that they were safe from the police,
12 _____ others created alibis by appearing in different places.
13 _____ came from outside the island.
14 _____, I was able to tell the police what had really happened

7   What were the motives for the different crimes and murders in these stories? Choose a motive (or more than one) to fit each name, and then write a sentence or two for each character, giving the reasons for your choice of motive.

MOTIVES		CHARACTERS	
fear	*madness*	Mark	Fred
revenge	*greed*	Celia	Susan
jealousy	*laziness*	Lucille	the Russians
desire for power		Holly Ann	

8   Here are some different titles for the stories. Which titles suit which stories? Some can go with more than one story. Which are they?

One Brave Act	Steps Towards Death
An Easy Job	The Rich and The Hungry
Keeping Death Alive	Memories Don't Die
A Better Way to Get Money	Laying a Trail to Death
Bad Dreams Forever	Death Waits at the Window
Not Guilty?	A Death in the Family

9   Discuss your answers to these questions.

   • Very few of the criminals in these stories are brought to justice or punished. Do you prefer crime stories that end like this, or stories with 'unsolved' crimes or more open endings? Why?

   • In your opinion, which was the most skilful murder (or crime) or the cleverest murderer (or criminal) in these stories?

   • Did the authors make you feel sympathetic towards any of these criminals? If so, which ones and why?

ABOUT THE AUTHORS

LAWRENCE BLOCK

Lawrence Block was born in 1938 and lives in New York. He has won various awards, including the Mystery Writers of America Edgar Award, and has written two popular series of crime novels. One features the ex-cop Matt Scudder, played in the film *Eight Million Ways to Die* by Jeff Bridges; the other is about Bernie Rhodenbarr, a burglar who solves crimes.

STANLEY ELLIN

Stanley Ellin was born in New York in 1916 and died there in 1986. He was a teacher, a steelworker, and a farmer before taking up writing. He is best known for his short stories, particularly his first, *The Specialty of the House*, about a New York restaurant with a special treat for its customers. He won the Mystery Writers of America Edgar Award three times, followed by the Grand Master Award for lifetime achievement.

DASHIELL HAMMETT

Hammett was born in Maryland in 1894, and died in 1961. For some years he worked for the famous Pinkerton's Detective Agency, where he learned much that he later used in his writing. His first short stories appeared in the magazine *Black Mask*, and his first famous novel was *The Maltese Falcon*, which introduced his private eye, Sam Spade. Other well-known titles are *The Glass Key* and *The Thin Man*.

PATRICIA HIGHSMITH

Patricia Highsmith was born in Texas in 1921 and grew up in New York, but lived much of her life in Europe. Her first book,

Strangers on a Train, was filmed by Alfred Hitchcock in 1951. She is best known for psychological thrillers, such as *The Blunderer*, *The Glass Cell*, *The Talented Mr Ripley*, *Found in the Street*, and *Edith's Diary*. She died in Switzerland in 1995.

JOHN LUTZ

John Lutz was born in Dallas, Texas, in 1939. He worked as a builder and a truck driver before becoming a writer. He has written dozens of short stories and writes under many names. His best-known private eye is Nudger, a real loser who is surrounded by problems – bills to pay, clients who won't pay him, and an ex-wife who wants everything she can get. If something can go wrong for Nudger, it will go wrong.

NANCY PICKARD

Nancy Pickard was born in 1945 and lives in Kansas with her husband and son. She has won awards for her novels and short stories and has written a series of crime novels featuring Jenny Cain. The Jenny Cain novels, she says, 'have three jobs: to entertain; to show what it's like to be a woman in the US now; and to allow the writer to work in and experiment with the mystery novel.'

MARY ROBERTS RINEHART

Rinehart was born in Pittsburgh, Pennsylvania, in 1876, and married a doctor when she was nineteen. In 1903 the American financial markets crashed, and the Rineharts were left heavily in debt. Mary began writing stories to make some money, and her first book, *The Circular Staircase*, appeared in 1908. She wrote twenty mystery novels and many short stories, and was at one time the highest-paid author in America. She died in 1958.

OXFORD BOOKWORMS LIBRARY

Classics • Crime & Mystery • Factfiles • Fantasy & Horror
Human Interest • Playscripts • Thriller & Adventure
True Stories • World Stories

The OXFORD BOOKWORMS LIBRARY provides enjoyable reading in English, with a wide range of classic and modern fiction, non-fiction, and plays. It includes original and adapted texts in seven carefully graded language stages, which take learners from beginner to advanced level. An overview is given on the next pages.

All Stage 1 titles are available as audio recordings, as well as over eighty other titles from Starter to Stage 6. All Starters and many titles at Stages 1 to 4 are specially recommended for younger learners. Every Bookworm is illustrated, and Starters and Factfiles have full-colour illustrations.

The OXFORD BOOKWORMS LIBRARY also offers extensive support. Each book contains an introduction to the story, notes about the author, a glossary, and activities. Additional resources include tests and worksheets, and answers for these and for the activities in the books. There is advice on running a class library, using audio recordings, and the many ways of using Oxford Bookworms in reading programmes. Resource materials are available on the website <www.oup.com/elt/gradedreaders>.

The *Oxford Bookworms Collection* is a series for advanced learners. It consists of volumes of short stories by well-known authors, both classic and modern. Texts are not abridged or adapted in any way, but carefully selected to be accessible to the advanced student.

You can find details and a full list of titles in the *Oxford Bookworms Library Catalogue* and *Oxford English Language Teaching Catalogues*, and on the website <www.oup.com/elt/gradedreaders>.

THE OXFORD BOOKWORMS LIBRARY
GRADING AND SAMPLE EXTRACTS

STARTER • 250 HEADWORDS

present simple – present continuous – imperative –
can/cannot, must – *going to* (future) – simple gerunds …

Her phone is ringing – but where is it?

Sally gets out of bed and looks in her bag. No phone. She looks under the bed. No phone. Then she looks behind the door. There is her phone. Sally picks up her phone and answers it. *Sally's Phone*

STAGE 1 • 400 HEADWORDS

… past simple – coordination with *and, but, or* –
subordination with *before, after, when, because, so* …

I knew him in Persia. He was a famous builder and I worked with him there. For a time I was his friend, but not for long. When he came to Paris, I came after him – I wanted to watch him. He was a very clever, very dangerous man. *The Phantom of the Opera*

STAGE 2 • 700 HEADWORDS

… present perfect – *will* (future) – *(don't) have to, must not, could* –
comparison of adjectives – simple *if* clauses – past continuous –
tag questions – *ask/tell* + infinitive …

While I was writing these words in my diary, I decided what to do. I must try to escape. I shall try to get down the wall outside. The window is high above the ground, but I have to try. I shall take some of the gold with me – if I escape, perhaps it will be helpful later. *Dracula*

STAGE 3 • 1000 HEADWORDS

... *should, may* – present perfect continuous – *used to* – past perfect – causative – relative clauses – indirect statements ...

Of course, it was most important that no one should see Colin, Mary, or Dickon entering the secret garden. So Colin gave orders to the gardeners that they must all keep away from that part of the garden in future. *The Secret Garden*

STAGE 4 • 1400 HEADWORDS

... past perfect continuous – passive (simple forms) – *would* conditional clauses – indirect questions – relatives with *where/when* – gerunds after prepositions/phrases ...

I was glad. Now Hyde could not show his face to the world again. If he did, every honest man in London would be proud to report him to the police. *Dr Jekyll and Mr Hyde*

STAGE 5 • 1800 HEADWORDS

... future continuous – future perfect – passive (modals, continuous forms) – *would have* conditional clauses – modals + perfect infinitive ...

If he had spoken Estella's name, I would have hit him. I was so angry with him, and so depressed about my future, that I could not eat the breakfast. Instead I went straight to the old house. *Great Expectations*

STAGE 6 • 2500 HEADWORDS

... passive (infinitives, gerunds) – advanced modal meanings – clauses of concession, condition

When I stepped up to the piano, I was confident. It was as if I knew that the prodigy side of me really did exist. And when I started to play, I was so caught up in how lovely I looked that I didn't worry how I would sound. *The Joy Luck Club*

119

BOOKWORMS · THRILLER & ADVENTURE · STAGE 6

Night Without End

ALISTAIR MACLEAN

Retold by Margaret Naudi

On the Polar ice-cap, 640 kilometres north of the Arctic Circle, the deadly, icy winds can freeze a man to death in minutes. But the survivors of the crashed airliner are lucky – they are rescued by three scientists from a nearby weather station.

But why did the airliner crash in the first place? Who smashed the radio to pieces? And why does the dead pilot have a bullet hole in his back? The rescue quickly turns into a nightmare: a race through the endless Arctic night, a race against time, cold, hunger – and a killer with a gun.

BOOKWORMS · CLASSICS · STAGE 6

Pride and Prejudice

JANE AUSTEN

Retold by Clare West

'The moment I first met you, I noticed your pride, your sense of superiority, and your selfish disdain for the feelings of others. You are the last man in the world whom I could ever be persuaded to marry,' said Elizabeth Bennet.

And so Elizabeth rejects the proud Mr Darcy. Can nothing overcome her prejudice against him? And what of the other Bennet girls – their fortunes, and misfortunes, in the business of getting husbands?

This famous novel by Jane Austen is full of wise and humorous observation of the people and manners of her times.